WE BELIEVE

A Comprehensive Statement of Christian Faith

Prepared by Ralph M. Riggs

GOSPEL PUBLISHING HOUSE
Springfield, Missouri
02-0780

This book is a combination of four booklets on the themes Elementary Bible History, Elementary Christian Doctrine, Adult Christian Doctrine, and Manual for Christian Living.

Printed in the United States of America

*The whole world lieth in wickedness
[the Wicked One]* (1 John 5:19).
*Having the understanding darkened,
being alienated from the life of God
through the ignorance that is in them*
(Ephesians 4:18). *The entrance of thy
words giveth light* (Psalm 119:130).
In thy light shall we see light (Psalm
36:9). *O send out thy light and thy
truth; let them lead me* (Psalm 43:3).

Introduction

The measure of salvation and spiritual light that has come to the world and to us individually is the measure in which the Word of God has been received. The measure of darkness and need which still exists anywhere is the measure in which the Word of God has not yet been received, believed, and appropriated. The supreme business, then, of gospel workers is to spread the gospel light. Not just an initial proclamation but a continual "line upon line, precept upon precept, here a little, there a little."

The word that Jesus saves, heals, baptizes in the Holy Spirit, and is coming soon has kindled a fire in the world and created the modern Pentecostal Movement. But these are "lines" of Scripture. "All scripture is given by inspiration of God, and is profitable for doctrine, for reproof, for correction, for instruction in righteousness: that the man of God may be perfect, thoroughly furnished unto all good works" (2 Timothy 3:16, 17). We all need to be "rooted and built up in him, and stablished in the faith" (Colossians 2:7). For our protection from the winds of false doctrine, for our defense against temptation of every kind, for our tapping the deep hidden springs of spiritual life and power, we all need to learn more and more of the precious Word of God.

This book has been prepared so that children and adults can become familiar with the Word of God. It is not an exhaustive study but simple courses of study which systematically cover all the doctrines of the Bible and the important facts of Bible history.

The courses are in question-and-answer form and cover the doctrines of the Christian faith, the Bible story from creation to the new heavens and the new earth, and practical Christian living. They also include some Bible book studies.

There are four parts. The first two are prepared especially for children, and the last two for adults. Part 1 contains facts about the Bible and Bible history. Part 2 centers on doctrine and Christian living. The adult section contains a comprehensive statement of Christian faith in Part 3 and a manual for Christian living and studies of Bible books in Part 4.

The uses for this book are limited only by the imagination of the teacher or leader. Here are some ideas:
1. Sunday school
2. New converts class
3. Vacation Bible school
4. Children's camp
5. Youth camps
6. Family worship
7. Home Bible studies
8. Home Bible clubs

The portions of verses or answers printed in italics (*this type*) are suggested for memorization.

Contents

Part 1: Bible History for Children

Part 2: Bible Doctrine, Christian Living for Children

A. Doctrine

MORE ▶

B. Christian Living

Part 3: Bible Doctrine for Adults

Part 4: Christian Living, Bible Book Studies for Adults

A. Christian Living

B. Bible Book Studies

PART 1
Bible History for Children

I. CREATION

1. Who made the world?

A. *God created the heaven and the earth.*

"In the beginning God created the heaven and the earth." Genesis 1:1.

2. How long did it take God to create the heaven and the earth?

A. *God created the heaven and the earth in six days.*

"And God saw everything that he had made, and, behold, it was very good. And the evening and the morning were the sixth day." Genesis 1:31.

3. What did God do on the seventh day?

A. *God rested on the seventh day.*

"And on the seventh day God ended his work which he had made; and he rested on the seventh day from all his work which he had made. And God blessed the seventh day, and sanctified it: because that in it he had rested from all his work which God created and made." Genesis 2:2, 3.

4. What did God create on the first day?

A. *God created light on the first day.*

"And God said, Let there be light: and there was light. And God saw the light, that it was good: and God divided the light from the darkness. God called the light Day, and the darkness he called Night. And the evening and the morning were the first day." Genesis 1:3-5.

5. What did God create on the second day?

A. *God made the heaven on the second day.*

"God made the firmament, and divided the waters which were under the firmament from the waters which were above the firmament: and it was so. And God called the firmament Heaven. And the evening and the morning were the second day." Genesis 1:7, 8.

3

6. What did God do about the waters under the heaven?

A. God gathered the waters under the heaven into one place and caused the dry land to appear.

"*God said, Let the waters under the heaven be gathered together unto one place, and let the dry land appear: and it was so. And God called the dry land Earth; and the gathering together of the waters called he Seas: and God saw that it was good.*" Genesis 1:9-10.

7. What did God command the earth to do?

A. God commanded the earth to bring forth all kinds of vegetation.

"*And God said, Let the earth bring forth grass, the herb yielding seed, and the fruit tree yielding fruit after his kind, whose seed is in itself, upon the earth: and it was so.*" Genesis 1:11.

8. What happened on the fourth day of creation?

A. God made the sun, moon and stars and put them in the heaven to give light upon the earth.

"*And God said, Let there be lights in the firmament of the heaven to divide the day from the night; and let them be for signs, and for seasons, for days, and years: and God made two great lights; the greater light to rule the day, and the lesser light to rule the night: He made the stars also. And God set them in the firmament of the heaven to give light upon the earth.*" Genesis 1:14, 16,17.

9. When did God make all living creatures?

A. God made every living creature on the fifth and sixth days.

"God created great whales, and every living creature that moveth, which the waters brought forth abundantly, after their kind, and every winged fowl after his kind: and God saw that it was good." "And God said, Let the earth bring forth the living creature after his kind, cattle and creeping thing, and beast of the earth after his kind: and it was so." Genesis 1:21, 24.

10. How did God make Adam?

A. God created Adam out of the dust of the ground and gave him a living soul.

"God formed Adam out of the dust of the ground, and breathed into his nostrils the breath of life; and man became a living soul." Genesis 2:7.

11. Whom did God create for Adam's helper and companion?

A. God created a woman and gave her to Adam for his wife.

"And the Lord God said, It is not good that the man should be alone; I will make him an help meet for him." Genesis 2:18.

12. How was Eve made?

A. God caused a deep sleep to fall upon Adam, and while he slept God took one of his ribs and made woman out of it.

"And the Lord God caused a deep sleep to fall upon Adam, and he slept; and he took one of his ribs, and closed up the flesh instead thereof; and the rib, which the Lord God had taken from man, made he a woman, and brought her unto the man." Genesis 2:21, 22.

13. Whom did God place in charge of all that He had created?

A. *God placed Adam and Eve in charge of all the earth.*

"God created man in his own image, in the image of God created he him; male and female created he them. And God blessed them, and God said unto them, be fruitful, and multiply, and replenish the earth, and subdue it: and have dominion over the fish of the sea, and over the fowl of the air, and over every living thing that moveth upon the earth." Genesis 1:27, 28.

14. Where did Adam and Eve live?

A. *Adam and Eve lived in the beautiful Garden of Eden that God had made for them.*

"And the Lord God planted a garden eastward in Eden; and there he put the man whom he had formed." Genesis 2:8.

15. What one thing did God command Adam and Eve not to do?

A. *God commanded them not to eat of the tree of knowledge of good and evil.*

"The Lord God commanded the man, saying, Of every tree of the garden thou mayest freely eat: but of the tree of the knowledge of good and evil, thou shalt not eat of it." Genesis 2:16, 17.

16. What did God say would happen to Adam if he ate of this tree of knowledge?

A. God told Adam if he ate of this tree he would surely die.

"*In the day that thou eatest thereof thou shalt surely die.*" Genesis 2:17.

17. Did Adam and Eve obey God?

A. *No. They disobeyed God and ate of the tree of the knowledge of good and evil.*

"And when the woman saw that the tree was good for food, and that it was pleasant to the eyes, and a tree to be desired to make one wise, she took of the fruit thereof, and did eat, and gave also unto her husband with her; and he did eat." Genesis 3:6.

18. Why did Adam and Eve disobey God and eat of the forbidden tree?

A. *Satan came in the form of a beautiful serpent and tempted Eve to eat of the forbidden tree.*

"And the serpent said unto the woman, Ye shall not surely die: for God doth know that in the day ye eat thereof, then your eyes shall be opened, and ye shall be as gods, knowing good and evil." Genesis 3:4, 5.

19. What happened when Adam and Eve disobeyed God?

A. *The sentence of death was placed upon them. God drove them from the garden of Eden. Adam had to work the ground for a living. The ground was cursed and thorns and thistles sprang up. Eve's sorrow was increased. The serpent was cursed and made to crawl on the ground and eat dust.*

"For . . . in Adam all die." 1 Corinthians 15:22.

20. What promise did God make in Genesis 3:15?

A. *God promised to send a Saviour to the world to redeem man from the curse of sin and death.*

"I will put enmity between thee and the woman, and between thy seed and her seed; it shall bruise thy head, and thou shalt bruise his heel." Genesis 3:15. "In Christ shall all be made alive." 1 Corinthians 15:22.

21. What awful thing happened in the family of Adam and Eve?

A. *Their firstborn, Cain, killed their second son, Abel.*

"And Cain talked with Abel his brother: and it came to pass, when they were in the field, that Cain rose up against Abel his brother, and slew him." Genesis 4:8.

22. Why did Cain kill Abel?

A. *Cain was angry because God had accepted Abel's offering of a slain lamb and had rejected his offering of the fruit of the ground.*

"And in process of time it came to pass, that Cain brought of the fruit of the ground an offering unto the Lord. And Abel, he also brought of the firstlings of his flock and of the fat thereof. And the Lord had respect unto Abel and to his offering: But unto Cain and to his offering he had not respect. And Cain was very wroth, and his countenance fell." Genesis 4:3-5.

23. Why did God accept Abel's offering and reject Cain's?

A. *God accepted Abel's offering because a slain lamb was a true type of the coming Redeemer whose shed blood would atone for the sins of the world. God rejected Cain's offering because it did not show that Cain honored God in his heart.*

"The next day John seeth Jesus coming unto him, and saith, Behold the Lamb of God, which taketh away the sin of the world." John 1:29.

"For this is the message that ye heard from the beginning, that we should love one another. Not as Cain, who was of that wicked one, and slew his brother. And wherefore slew he him? Because his own works were evil, and his brother's righteous." 1 John 3:11, 12.

24. Who was Enoch?

A. *Enoch was a good man who was translated and went to heaven without dying.*

"And Enoch also, the seventh from Adam, prophesied of these, saying, Behold, the Lord cometh with ten thousands of his saints." Jude 14.

"*By faith Enoch was translated that he should not see death*; and was not found, because God had translated him: *for before his translation he had this testimony, that he pleased God." Hebrews* 11:5.

II. THE FLOOD

1. Who was Noah?

A. *Noah was a just man who lived in the tenth generation after Adam.*

"Noah was a just man and perfect in his generations, and Noah walked with God." Genesis 6:9.

2. Who were the sons of Noah?

A. *The sons of Noah were Shem, Ham, and Japheth.*

"Noah begat three sons, Shem, Ham, and Japheth." Genesis 6:10.

3. What were the conditions on the earth at the time Noah lived?

A. *The wickedness of man was very great. Noah and his family were the only righteous people.*
"And God saw that the wickedness of man was great in the earth, and that every imagination of the thoughts of his heart was only evil continually. . . . But Noah found grace in the eyes of the Lord." Genesis 6:5, 8.

4. What did this wickedness cause God to do?

A. *God said that He would destroy man from the earth because of his wickedness.*
"The Lord said, I will destroy man whom I have created from the face of the earth; both man, and beast, and the creeping thing, and the fowls of the air; for it repenteth me that I have made them." Genesis 6:7.

5. What did God tell Noah to do?

A. *God told Noah to build an ark, for He was going to send a flood to destroy all flesh.*
"Make thee an ark of gopher wood; rooms shalt thou make in the ark, and shalt pitch it within and without with pitch. . . . Behold, I . . . do bring a flood of waters upon the earth, to destroy all flesh." Genesis 6:14, 17.

6. How long did Noah warn the people of the coming judgment?

A. *Noah warned the people of the coming judgment for 120 years.*
"And the Lord said, My spirit shall not always strive with man, for that he also is flesh: yet his days shall be an hundred and twenty years." Genesis 6:3.

7. Who did Noah take with him in the ark when it was finished?

A. *Noah took his wife and three sons and their wives and two of every kind of animal that was on the earth.*
"With thee will I establish my covenant; and thou shalt come into the ark, thou, and thy sons, and thy wife, and thy sons' wives with thee. And of every living thing of all flesh, two of every sort shalt thou

bring into the ark, to keep them alive with thee; they shall be male and female." Genesis 6:18, 19.

8. What happened when God shut the door of the ark?

A. *The rain came as Noah had warned and every living thing was destroyed from off the earth, except those who were in the ark.*

"In the six hundreth year of Noah's life, in the second month, the seventeenth day of the month, the same day were all the fountains of the great deep broken up, and the windows of heaven were opened. And every living substance was destroyed which was upon the face of the ground, both man, and cattle, and the creeping things, and the fowl of the heaven; and they were destroyed from the earth: and Noah only remained alive, and they that were with him in ark." Genesis 7:11, 23.

9. What was the first thing that Noah did when he came out of the ark after the waters had gone down?

A. *Noah built an altar unto the Lord and worshiped Him.*

"Noah went forth, and his sons, and his wife, and his sons' wives with him. And Noah builded an altar unto the Lord, . . . and offered burnt offerings on the altar." Genesis 8:18, 20.

10. What covenant did God make with Noah?

A. *God told Noah that never again would He destroy the earth by a flood.* He also gave them flesh to eat but forbade the eating of blood.

"But flesh with the life thereof, which is the blood thereof, shall ye not eat." Genesis 9:4.
"Behold, I establish my covenant with you, and with your seed after you; neither shall all flesh be cut off any more by the waters of a flood; neither shall there any more be a flood to destroy the earth." Genesis 9:9, 11.

11. What was the sign of God's promise to Noah and his sons?

A. *God set the rainbow in the heavens as a sign of His promise to Noah and his sons.*

"I do set my bow in the cloud, and it shall be for a token of a covenant between me and the earth." Genesis 9:13.

12. Did the descendants of Noah remain true to God?

A. No. They determined to build a city and a tower whose top would reach to heaven.

"And they said, Go to, let us build us a city and a tower, whose top may reach unto heaven; and let us make us a name, lest we be scattered abroad upon the face of the whole earth." Genesis 11:4.

13. What happened to the builders of the tower of Babel?

A. *God mixed their language so that they did not understand one another's speech. This is the origin of the many languages used on the earth today.*

"Go to, let us go down, and there confound their language, that they may not understand one another's speech." Genesis 11:7.

III. THE PATRIARCHS

1. Who was Abraham?

A. *Abraham was a righteous man who lived in the tenth generation after Noah.*

"And Terah lived seventy years, and begat Abram . . ." *Genesis 11:26*

"Abraham believed God, and it was counted unto him for righteousness." *Romans 4:3.*

2. What was God's promise to Abraham?

A. *God promised to give him and his children the land of Canaan and that he would become a father of many nations and that through him all the nations of the earth would be blessed.*

"Neither shall thy name any more be called Abram, but thy name shall be Abraham; for a father of many nations have I made thee. And I will give unto thee and to thy seed after thee, the land wherein thou art a stranger, all the land of Canaan, for an everlasting possession; and I will be their God. And in thy seed shall all the nations of the earth be blessed; because thou hast obeyed my voice." Genesis 17:5, 8; 22:18.

3. How did God plan to bless all the nations of the earth through Abraham?

A. *God planned to send a Redeemer to the earth who would be a descendant of Abraham.*

"Now to Abraham and his seed were the promises made. He saith not, And to seeds, as of many; but as of one, And to thy seed, which is Christ." Galatians 3:16.

4. Who was Isaac?

A. *Isaac was Abraham's son* to whom God promised to establish the covenant which He had made to Abraham.

"God said, Sarah thy wife shall bear thee a son indeed; and thou shalt call his name Isaac: and I will establish my covenant with him for an everlasting covenant, and with his seed after him." Genesis 17:19.

5. Who were the sons of Isaac?

A. *Jacob and Esau were twin sons of Isaac.*

"They called his name Esau . . . and his brother . . . was called Jacob." Genesis 25:25, 26.

6. Which of Isaac's sons received the promised blessing of their grandfather, Abraham?

A. *Jacob was the son who inherited the promised blessing.*

"And Isaac called Jacob, and blessed him. . . . God Almighty bless thee, and make thee fruitful, and multiply thee, that thou mayest be a multitude of people; and give thee the blessing of Abraham, to thee, and to thy seed with thee; that thou mayest inherit the land wherein thou art a stranger, which God gave unto Abraham." Genesis 28:1, 3, 4.

7. How many sons did Jacob have?

A. *Jacob had twelve sons whose descendants became the twelve tribes of Israel.*

"Now the sons of Jacob were twelve: Reuben, Simeon, Levi, Judah, Issachar, Zebulun, Joseph, Benjamin, Dan, Naphtali, Gad and Asher." Genesis 35:22, 23, 24, 25, and 26.

IV. EGYPT

1. Who was Joseph?

A. *Joseph was the favorite son of Jacob.*

"Now Israel loved Joseph more than all his children, because he was the son of his old age: and he made him a coat of many colors." Genesis 37:3.

2. How did Joseph get down to Egypt?

A. *He was sold by his brethren to traveling merchants who took him down to Egypt.*

"Then there passed by Midianites merchantmen; and they drew and lifted up Joseph out of the pit, and sold Joseph to the Ishmeelites for twenty pieces of silver: and they brought Joseph into Egypt." Genesis 37:28.

3. What happened to Joseph in Egypt?

A. *After many years of trial, Joseph became next to Pharaoh, the King of Egypt, in authority.*

"And Pharaoh said unto his servants, Can we find such a one as this is, a man in whom the Spirit of God is? Thou shalt be over my house, and according unto thy word shall all my people be ruled: only in the throne will I be greater than thou." Genesis 41: 38, 40.

4. What caused Joseph's brethren to come down into Egypt?

A. *There was a famine and they went to Egypt to buy corn.*

"Now when Jacob saw that there was corn in Egypt, Jacob said unto his sons, Why do ye look one upon another? And he said, Behold, I have heard that there is corn in Egypt: get you down thither, and buy for us from thence; that we may live, and not die. And Joseph's ten brethren went down to buy corn in Egypt." Genesis 42:1-3.

5. What happened to Joseph's brothers when they came to Egypt?

A. *They were brought before Joseph,* and they were afraid of him.

"And Joseph was the governor over the land, and he it was that sold to all the people of the land: and Joseph's brethren came, and bowed down themselves before him with their faces to the earth." Genesis 42:6. "And Joseph said unto his brethren, I am Joseph; doth my father yet live? And his brethren could not answer him; for they were troubled at his presence." Genesis 45:3.

6. What did Joseph do to his brothers?

A. *He gave them food and was kind to them.* He sent for his father, Jacob, and they all lived there in Egypt with Joseph.

"Haste ye, and go up to my father, and say unto him, Thus saith thy son Joseph, God hath made me lord of all Egypt: come down unto me, tarry not: And thou shalt dwell in the land of Goshen, and thou shalt be near unto me, thou, and thy children, and thy children's children, and thy flocks, and thy herds, and all that thou hast: and there will I nourish thee; for yet there are five years of famine; lest thou and thy household, and all that thou hast, come to poverty." Genesis 45:9-11.

7. How long were the children of Israel in Egypt?

A. *They were there four hundred and thirty years.*

"And it came to pass at the end of the four hundred and thirty years, even the selfsame day it came to pass, that all the hosts of the Lord went out from the land of Egypt." Exodus 12:41.

8. What happened to the children of Israel while they were in Egypt?

A. *They became slaves to the Egyptians.*

"And the Egyptians made the children of Israel to serve with rigour: and they made their lives bitter with hard bondage, in morter, and in brick, and in all manner of service in the field: all their service, wherein they made them serve, was with rigour." Exodus 1:13-14.

9. Did God do anything to help the children of Israel?

A. *Yes, God sent Moses to lead them out of Egypt.*

"Come now therefore, and I will send thee unto Pharaoh, that thou mayest bring forth my people the children of Israel out of Egypt." Exodus 3:10.

10. What did God do to make the Egyptians willing to let the children of Israel go?

A. *God sent plagues on the Egyptians. He finally slew all of their firstborn children. Only those who killed a lamb and sprinkled its blood on the doorposts of their homes escaped.*

"And all the firstborn in the land of Egypt shall die, from the firstborn of Pharaoh that sitteth upon his throne, even unto the firstborn of the maidservant that is behind the mill; and all the firstborn of beasts. And the blood shall be to you for a token upon the houses where ye are: and when I see the blood, I will pass over you, and the plague shall not be upon you to destroy you, when I smite the land of Egypt." Exodus 11:5; 12:13.

11. What was the killing of the lamb and the sprinkling of blood on the doorposts called?

A. *It was called the Passover.*

"That ye shall say, It is the sacrifice of the Lord's passover, who passed over the houses of the children of Israel in Egypt, when he smote the Egyptians, and delivered our houses." Exodus 12:27.

12. Of what is the Passover a type?

A. *It is a type of Jesus' shed blood which will save all those who come to Him.*

"And it shall be for a sign unto thee upon thine hand, and for a memorial between thine eyes, that the Lord's law may be in thy mouth: for with a strong hand hath the Lord brought thee out of Egypt." Exodus 13:9.

"How much more shall the blood of Christ, who through the eternal Spirit offered himself without spot to God, purge your conscience from dead works to serve the living God?" Hebrews 9:14.

"Purge out therefore the old leaven, that ye may be a new lump, as ye are unleavened. For even Christ our passover is sacrificed for us." 1 Corinthians 5:7.

13. How else did God show the children of Israel He was with them?

A. *God performed many miracles. He divided the waters of the Red Sea so they could pass over on dry land. He sent them a pillar of cloud by day and of fire by night to lead them.*

"And the Lord went before them by day in a pillar of a cloud, to lead them the way; and by night in a pillar of fire, to give them light; to go by day and night: He took not away the pillar of the cloud by day, nor the pillar of fire by night, from before the people." Exodus 13:21, 22.

"And Moses stretched out his hand over the sea; and the Lord caused the sea to go back by a strong east wind all that night, and made the sea dry land, and the waters were divided. And the children of Israel went into the midst of the sea upon the dry ground. Exodus 14:21, 22a

14. What important event happened at Mt. Sinai?

A. *God gave Moses the Ten Commandments written on tablets of stone.*

"And Moses turned, and went down from the mount, and the two tables of the testimony were in his hand:

the tables were written on both their sides; on the
one side and on the other were they written.   And
the tables were the work of God, and the writing
was the writing of God, graven upon the tables."
Exodus 32:15, 16.

**15. What did the children of Israel do when they reached
the border of Canaan?**

A. *They sent twelve spies into Canaan to see
what the land and the people were like.*
"Send thou men, that they may search the land of
Canaan, which I give unto the children of Israel: of
every tribe of their fathers shall ye send a man, every
one a ruler among them." Numbers 13:2.

16. What report did these spies bring back?

A. *They said it was a land flowing with milk
and honey, but ten of the spies said there were
giants in the land who could not be conquered.   Only two of the spies (Caleb and
Joshua) gave a good report.*   They said: We
are well able to possess the land, for God is
with us!
"And they went and came to Moses, and to Aaron, and
to all the congregation of the children of Israel, unto
the wilderness of Paran, to Kadesh; and brought back
word unto them, and unto all the congregation, and
shewed them the fruit of the land.   And they told
him, and said, We came unto the land whither thou
sentest us, and surely it floweth with milk and honey;
and this is the fruit of it. Nevertheless the people be
strong that dwell in the land, and the cities are walled,
and very great: and moreover we saw the children of
Anak there.   The Amalekites dwell in the land of the
south: and the Hittites, and the Jebusites and the
Amorites, dwell in the mountains: and the Canaanites
dwell by the sea, and by the coast of Jordan. And
Caleb stilled the people before Moses, and said, Let
us go up at once, and possess it; for ye are well
able to overcome it.   But the men that went up
with him said, We be not able to go up against the
people; for they are stronger than we." Numbers
13:26-31.

17. Did the children of Israel believe Caleb and Joshua?

A. *No. They did not believe their report. They did not enter into the Promised Land because they did not have faith in God.*

"So we see that they could not enter in because of unbelief." Hebrews 3:19.

18. How did God punish the children of Israel for their unbelief?

A. *God left them to wander in the wilderness for forty years.* All except Caleb and Joshua and those under 20 years of age died in the wilderness.

"Your carcases shall fall in this wilderness; and all that were numbered of you, according to your whole number, from twenty years old and upward, which have murmured against me." Numbers 14:29.

19. Whom did God choose to lead the children of Israel into Canaan, the Promised Land, after Moses' death?

A. *Joshua led the children of Israel into Canaan, or the Promised Land.*

"Now after the death of Moses the servant of the Lord it came to pass, that the Lord spake unto Joshua the son of Nun, Moses' minister, saying, Moses my servant is dead; now therefore arise, go over this Jordan, thou, and all this people, unto the land which I do give to them, even to the children of Israel. Every place that the sole of your foot shall tread upon, that have I given unto you, as I said unto Moses." Joshua 1:1-3.

V. JUDGES

1. What happened when the Israelites went into Canaan?

A. *They conquered its inhabitants and dwelt in their cities.*

"And the Lord gave them rest round about, according to all that he sware unto their fathers: and there stood not a man of all their enemies before them; the Lord delivered all their enemies into their hand." Joshua 21:44.

2. Did the Israelites remain true to God?

A. *No. The children of Israel disobeyed God over and over. As a result God let their enemies overcome them. Then in answer to prayers of repentance, God raised up men to deliver them from their enemies. These men were called Judges.*

"And also all that generation were gathered unto their fathers: and there arose another generation after them, which knew not the Lord, nor yet the works which he had done for Israel. And the children of Israel did evil in the sight of the Lord, and served Baalim: and they forsook the Lord God of their fathers, which brought them out of the land of Egypt, and followed other gods, of the gods of the people that were round about them, and bowed themselves unto them; and provoked the Lord to anger. Nevertheless the Lord raised up judges, which delivered them out of the hand of the those that spoiled them." Judges 2:10-12, 16.

3. How long did God rule the children of Israel through the Judges?

A. *The time of the Judges extended over a period of about four hundred and fifty years.*

"And after that he gave unto them judges about the space of four hundred and fifty years, until Samuel the prophet." Acts 13:20.

4. How many Judges were there in Israel, and which books of the Bible relate the history of Israel under these Judges?

A. *There were fourteen Judges.* The books of Judges and 1 Samuel relate the history of Israel under the Judges.

"And when the children of Israel cried unto the Lord, the Lord raised up a deliverer to the children of Israel, who delivered them, even Othniel the son of Kenaz, Caleb's younger brother. And the Spirit of the Lord came upon him, and he judged Israel, and went out to war: and the Lord delivered Chushan-risha-thaim king of Mesopotamia into his hand: and his hand

prevailed against Chushan-risha-thaim." Judges 3:9, 10.
"And all Israel from Dan even to Beer-sheba knew that
Samuel was established to be a prophet of the Lord."
1 Samuel 3:20.

5. Name some of the most outstanding Judges.

A. *Deborah, Gideon, Jephtha, Samson, and Sam-*
uel were some of the most outstanding Judges.

"And what shall I more say? for the time would fail
me to tell of Gedeon, and of Barak, and of Samson, and
Jephthae; of David also, and Samuel, and of the
prophets." Hebrews 11:32.

6. How was Deborah different from all the rest?

A. *Deborah was a woman Judge in Israel.*

"And Deborah, a prophetess, the wife of Lapidoth, she
judged Israel at that time." Judges 4:4.

VI. THE KINGS

1. Who ruled Israel after the Judges?

A. *God gave Israel kings to rule over them.*

"Tomorrow about this time I will send thee a man out
of the land of Benjamin, and thou shalt anoint him
to be captain over my people Israel, that he may save
my people out of the hand of the Philistines: for I
have looked upon my people, because their cry is come
unto me." 1 Samuel 9:16.

2. Who was Israel's first king?

A. *Saul was Israel's first king.*

"And when Samuel saw Saul, the Lord said unto him,
Behold the man whom I spake to thee of! This same
shall reign over my people." 1 Samuel 9:17.

3. Was Saul a good king?

A. *Saul was a good king at first, but he disobeyed*
God and God took the throne away from him.

"And Samuel said, When thou wast little in thine own
sight, was thou not made the head of the tribes of
Israel, and the Lord anointed thee king over Israel?

. . . Because thou hast rejected the word of the Lord, he hath also rejected thee from being king." 1 Samuel 15: 17, 23b.

4. Who was the second king of Israel?

A. *David was the second king of Israel.*

"Then Samuel took the horn of oil, and anointed him in the midst of his brethren: and the Spirit of the Lord came upon David from that day forward. So Samuel rose up, and went to Ramah." 1 Samuel 16:13.

5. Was David a good king?

A. *Yes. He was the best king Israel ever had.*

"And when he had removed him, he raised up unto them David to be their king; to whom also he gave testimony, and said, I have found David the son of Jesse, a man after mine own heart, which shall fulfill all my will." Acts 13:22.

6. What special promise did God make to David?

A. *God promised that the Messiah would be David's son.*

"And when thy days be fulfilled, and thou shalt sleep with thy fathers, I will set up thy seed after thee, which shall proceed out of thy bowels, and I will establish his kingdom. He shall build an house for my name, and I will stablish the throne of his kingdom for ever." 2 Sam. 7:12, 13.

"And when Jesus departed thence, two blind men followed him, crying and saying, Thou son of David, have mercy on us." Matthew 9:27.

7. Who succeeded David to the throne?

A. *Solomon, David's son, succeeded him to the throne.*

"And let Zadok the priest and Nathan the prophet anoint him there king over Israel: and blow ye with the trumpet, and say, God save king Solomon. Then ye shall come up after him, that he may come and sit upon my throne; for he shall be king in my stead: and I have appointed him to be ruler over Israel and over Judah." 1 Kings 1:34, 35.

8. What great choice did Solomon make that pleased God?

A. *Solomon asked God to give him wisdom and knowledge so that he could rule the people well.*

"Give therefore thy servant an understanding heart to judge thy people, that I may discern between good and bad: for who is able to judge this thy so great a people? And the speech pleased the Lord, that Solomon had asked this thing." 1 Kings 3:9, 10.

9. Did God grant Solomon's request?

A. *Yes. God gave him wisdom and knowledge above all else. He also gave him great honor and riches.*

"Behold, I have done according to thy words: lo, I have given thee a wise and an understanding heart; so that there was none like thee before thee, neither after thee shall any arise like unto thee. And I have also given thee that which thou hast not asked, both riches, and honour: so that there shall not be any among the kings like unto thee all thy days." 1 Kings 3:12, 13.

10. What did Solomon do for God?

A. *Solomon built a great temple (or church) at Jerusalem where the people came to worship God.*

"And, Behold, I purpose to build an house unto the name of the Lord my God, as the Lord spake unto David my father, saying, Thy son, whom I will set upon thy throne in thy room, he shall build an house unto my name." 1 Kings 5:5.

11. What happened to Israel after Solomon's death?

A. *The kingdom was divided. Two tribes remained true to King Rehoboam, Solomon's son, and were known as Judah. The other ten tribes revolted and chose Jeroboam, son of Nebat, Solomon's servant, as their king. They were known as Israel.*

"So when all Israel saw that the king hearkened not unto them, the people answered the king, saying, What

portion have we in David? neither have we inheritance
in the son of Jesse: to your tents, O Israel: now see
to thine own house, David.   So Israel departed unto
their tents.   But as for the children of Israel which
dwelt in the cities of Judah, Rehoboam reigned over
them. So Israel rebelled against the house of David
unto this day." 1 Kings 12:16, 17, 19.

**12. What happened to this divided kingdom, and what
books of the Bible contain its history?**

A. *There were many bad kings and some good
kings who ruled over each part of the divided
kingdom.   The history of Israel and Judah
may be found in 1 and 2 Kings and 1 and 2
Chronicles.*

13. How long did these kingdoms last?

A. *The kingdom of Israel continued for 253
years, and the kingdom of Judah continued
for 389 years.*

14. How did these kingdoms fall?

A. *Israel was captured by the Assyrians, and
Judah was captured by the Babylonians.*

"In the ninth year of Hoshea the king of Assyria took
Samaria, and carried Israel away into Assyria, and
placed them in Halah and in Habor by the river of
Gozan, and in the cities of the Medes." 2 Kings 17:6.
"And he carried away all Jerusalem, and all the
princes, and all the mighty men of valour, even ten
thousand captives, and all the craftsmen and smiths:
none remained, save the poorest sort of the people of
the land. And he carried away Jehoiachin to Babylon, and the king's mother, and the king's wives,
and his officers, and the mighty of the land, those
carried he into captivity from Jerusalem to Babylon.
And all the men of might, even seven thousand,
and craftsmen and smiths a thousand, all that were
strong and apt for war, even them the king of Babylon
brought captive to Babylon." 2 Kings 24:14-16.

15. What happened to the beautiful temple Solomon built?

A. *God allowed the armies of Nebuchadnezzar to destroy it.*

"And he burnt the house of the Lord, and the king's house, and all the houses of Jerusalem, and every great man's house burnt he with fire." 2 Kings 25:9.

16. How long did the Kingdom of Judah remain in captivity?

A. *Judah remained in Babylonian captivity for 70 years.*

"And this whole land shall be a desolation, and an astonishment; and these nations shall serve the king of Babylon seventy years." Jeremiah 25:11.

17. What became of the ten tribes of Israel?

A. *Many of the people of the ten tribes were taken into the two tribes under Judah, and the rest were absorbed into the nations where they lived.*

"Nevertheless divers of Asher and Manasseh and of Zebulun humbled themselves, and came to Jerusalem. For a multitude of the people, even many of Ephraim, and Manasseh, Issachar, and Zebulun, had not cleansed themselves, yet did they eat the passover otherwise than it was written. But Hezekiah prayed for them, saying, The good Lord pardon every one. And all the congregation of Judah, with the priests and the Levites, and all the congregation that came out of Israel, and the strangers that came out of the land of Israel, and that dwelt in Judah, rejoiced." 2 Chron. 30:11, 18, 25.

"And offered at the dedication of this house of God an hundred bullocks, two hundred rams, four hundreds lambs; and for a sin-offering for all Israel, twelve he goats, according to the number of the tribes of Israel." "Also the children of those that had been carried away, which were come out of the captivity, offered burnt-offerings unto the God of Israel, twelve bullocks for all Israel, ninety and six rams, seventy and seven lambs, twelve he goats for a sin-offering:

all this was a burnt-offering unto the Lord." Ezra
6:17; 8:35.

"Unto which promise our twelve tribes, instantly
serving God day and night, hope to come. For which
hope's sake, king Agrippa, I am accused of the Jews."
Acts 26:7.

"James, a servant of God and of the Lord Jesus Christ,
to the twelve tribes which are scattered abroad, greet-
ing." James 1:1.

**18. What did the Jews do when they returned to Jeru-
salem after their captivity?**

A. *They rebuilt the city and the temple that had
been destroyed.*

"And I said unto the king, If it please the king, and
if thy servant have found favor in thy sight, that thou
wouldest send me unto Judah, unto the city of my
fathers' sepulchres, that I may build it." "So built we
the wall; and all the wall was joined together unto
the half thereof: for the people had a mind to work."
Nehemiah 2:5; 4:6.

"And when the builders laid the foundation of the
temple of the Lord. And all the people shouted with
a great shout, when they praised the Lord, because
the foundation of the house of the Lord was laid."
Ezra 3:10a; 11b.

19. Were the Jews (Judah) a strong nation after that?

A. *No. They continued as a subject nation for
400 years until Christ came and afterward
on to their dispersion.*

"Now when Jesus was born in Bethlehem of Judea
in the days of Herod the king, behold, there came wise
men from the east to Jerusalem." Matthew 2:1.

VII.   THE PROPHETS

1. Who were the prophets?

A. *The prophets were preachers whom God called
to warn Israel of coming judgment.*

"Wherefore, behold, I send unto you prophets."
Matthew 23:34a.

"God, who at sundry times and in divers manners spake in times past unto the fathers by the prophets." Hebrews 1:1.

2. When did they preach, or prophesy?

A. *They preached during the reign of the kings,* also during and after the captivity of the children of Israel.

"And he sent Eliakim, which was over the household, and Shebna the scribe, and the elders of the priests, covered with sackcloth, to Isaiah the prophet the son of Amoz." 2 Kings 19:2.

"Then the prophets, Haggai the prophet, and Zechariah the son of Iddo, prophesied unto the Jews that were in Judah and Jerusalem in the name of the God of Israel, even unto them." Ezra 5:1.

3. What important future events did the prophets tell about?

A. *They told about the first and second comings of Christ.*

"The Spirit of the Lord God is upon me; because the Lord hath anointed me to preach good tidings unto the meek; he hath sent me to bind up the brokenhearted, to proclaim liberty to the captives, and the opening of the prison to them that are bound; to proclaim the acceptable year of the Lord, and the day of vengeance of our God; to comfort all that mourn." Isaiah 61:1, 2.

4. Have all these prophecies been fulfilled?

A. *The prophecies concerning the first coming of Christ were all fulfilled accurately. The prophecies concerning His second coming will also be fulfilled.*

"Now all this was done, that it might be fulfilled which was spoken of the Lord by the prophet." Matthew 1:22.

"For these things were done, that the scripture should be fulfilled, A bone of him shall not be broken." John 19:36.

VIII. THE LIFE OF CHRIST

1. Where was Jesus born?

A. *Jesus was born in a manger in Bethlehem of Judea,* because there was no room in the inn.

"And Joseph also went up from Galilee, out of the city of Nazareth, into Judea, unto the city of David, which is called Bethlehem; (because he was of the house and lineage of David;) . . . *And she brought forth her firstborn son, and wrapped him in swaddling clothes, and laid him in a manger; because there was no room for them in the inn." Luke* 2:4, 7.

2. Who were Jesus' parents?

A. *Mary was Jesus' mother and God was His father. Joseph was Jesus' foster father because he was married to Mary.*

"Now the birth of Jesus Christ was on this wise: When as his mother Mary was espoused to Joseph, before they came together, she was found with child of the Holy Ghost. Then Joseph her husband, being a just man, and not willing to make her a publick example, was minded to put her away privily. But while he thought on these things, behold, the angel of the Lord appeared unto him in a dream, saying, Joseph, thou son of David, fear not to take unto thee Mary thy wife: for that which is conceived in her is of the Holy Ghost. And she shall bring forth a son, and thou shalt call his name JESUS: for he shall save his people from their sins." Matthew 1:18-21.

3. Who were the first to worship Jesus?

A. *The Shepherds were the first to find the baby Jesus and worship Him.*

"And there were in the same country shepherds abiding in the field, keeping watch over their flock by night. And, lo, the angel of the Lord came upon them, and the glory of the Lord shone round about them: and they were sore afraid. And the angel said unto them, Fear not: for, behold, I bring you good tidings of great joy, which shall be to all people. For unto you is born this day in the city of David a Saviour, which is Christ the Lord. And this shall be a sign unto

you: Ye shall find the babe wrapped in swaddling clothes, lying in a manger. And suddenly there was with the angel a multitude of the heavenly host praising God, and saying: Glory to God in the highest, and on earth peace, good will toward men." Luke 2:8-14.

4. Who else came and worshiped Jesus?

A. *The Wise Men from the East came to worship Jesus.*

"Now when Jesus was born in Bethlehem of Judea in the days of Herod the king, behold, there came wise men from the east to Jerusalem, saying, Where is he that is born King of the Jews? For we have seen his star in the east, and come to worship him. . . . *And when they were come into the house, they saw the young child with Mary his mother, and fell down, and worshipped him." Matthew* 2:1, 2, 11.

5. How did they find Jesus?

A. *They saw His star in the east and followed it to the place where Jesus was.*

"The star, which they saw in the east, went before them, till it came and stood over where the young child was. Matthew 2:9.

6. Did they bring gifts to Jesus?

A. Yes. They brought Him gold, frankincense, and myrrh.

"*And when they had opened their treasures, they presented unto him gifts; gold, and frankincense, and myrrh."*

7. What did God warn Joseph in a dream to do?

A. *He warned Joseph to take Jesus and flee to Egypt because King Herod wanted to kill Jesus.*

"The angel of the Lord appeared to Joseph in a dream, saying, Arise, and take the young child and his mother, and flee into Egypt, and be thou there until I bring thee word: for Herod will seek the young child to destroy him." Matthew 2:13.

8. After the wicked King Herod died, where did Joseph take Mary and Jesus to live?

A. *They returned to the land of Israel and lived at Nazareth in Galilee.*

"And when they had performed all things according to the law of the Lord, they returned into Galilee, to their own city Nazareth." Luke 2:39.

9. What happened when Jesus was twelve years old?

A. *Jesus went with His parents to Jerusalem for the feast of the Passover. When Mary and Joseph had gone a day's journey on their way back home, they discovered that Jesus was not in their party. They returned to Jerusalem and after three days found Him in the temple talking to the doctors of the law.*

"Now his parents went to Jerusalem every year at the feast of the passover. And when he was twelve years old, they went up to Jerusalem after the custom of the feast. And when they had fulfilled the days, as they returned, the child Jesus tarried behind in Jerusalem: and Joseph and his mother knew not of it. But they, supposing him to have been in the company, went a day's journey; and they sought him among their kinsfolk and acquaintance. And when they found him not, they turned back again to Jerusalem, seeking him." Luke 2:41-45.

10. Do we have any record of what Jesus did between the ages of 12 and 30?

A. *We are told only that Jesus went down to Nazareth and was obedient to His parents* and that He grew, and increased in favor with God and man.

"And he went down with them, and came to Nazareth, and was subject unto them: but his mother kept all these sayings in her heart. *And Jesus increased in wisdom and stature and in favor with God and man.*" *Luke* 2:51, 52.

11. How did Jesus begin His ministry?

A. *He was baptized by John the Baptist in the River Jordan.*

"Then cometh Jesus from Galilee to Jordan unto John, to be baptized of him." Matthew 3:13.

12. How did God show that He was with Him?

A. As Jesus came up out of the water, the Holy Spirit descended on Him in the form of a dove, and a voice from heaven came saying, This is my beloved Son in whom I am well pleased.

"And Jesus, when he was baptized, went up straightway out of the water: and, lo, the heavens were opened unto him, and he saw the Spirit of God descending like a dove, and lighting upon him. And lo a voice from heaven, saying, This is my beloved Son, in whom I am well pleased." Matthew 3:16, 17.

13. What happened to Jesus after He was baptized?

A. *The Spirit led Him into the wilderness to be tempted of Satan.*

"Then was Jesus led up of the Spirit into the wilderness to be tempted of the devil." Matthew 4:1.

14. How did Jesus overcome Satan's temptations?

A. He overcame them by using the Word of God.

"But he answered and said, It is written, Man shall not live by bread alone, but by every word that proceedeth out of the mouth of God. Jesus said unto him, It is written again, Thou shalt not tempt the Lord thy God. Then saith Jesus unto him, Get thee hence, Satan: for it is written, Thou shalt worship the Lord thy God, and him only shalt thou serve." Matthew 4:4, 7, 10.

15. Name the twelve disciples whom Jesus called to be with Him.

A. *The twelve disciples are: "Simon, who is called Peter, and Andrew his brother; James the son of Zebedee, and John his brother; Philip, and Bartholomew; Thomas, and Matthew the publican; James the son of Alphaeus; and Lebbaeus, whose surname was Thaddaeus: Simon the Canaanite, and Judas Iscariot, who also betrayed him." Matthew 10:2-4.*

16. What was the first miracle Jesus performed?

A. *The first miracle Jesus performed was to turn the water into wine at the wedding in Cana.*

"This beginning of miracles did Jesus in Cana of Galilee, and manifested forth his glory; and his disciples believed on him." John 2:11.

17. Name different kinds of miracles which Jesus performed.

A. *He healed the sick, raised the dead, walked on the sea, stilled the tempest, and multiplied the loaves and fishes.*

"The blind receive their sight, and the lame walk, the lepers are cleansed, and the deaf hear, the dead are raised up, and the poor have the gospel preached to them." Matthew 11:5. "And Jesus took the loaves; and when he had given thanks, he distributed to the disciples, and the disciples to them that were set down; and likewise of the fishes as much as they would." John 6:11. "So when they had rowed about five and twenty or thirty furlongs, they see Jesus walking on the sea, and drawing nigh unto the ship: and they were afraid." John 6:19.

18. What was Jesus' favorite method of teaching?

A. *He spoke many parables, like the Good Samaritan and the Prodigal Son.*

"And he spake many things unto them in parables, saying, Behold, a sower went forth to sow." Matthew 13:3. "And Jesus answering said, A certain man went down from Jerusalem to Jericho, and fell among thieves, which stripped him of his raiment, and wounded him, and departed, leaving him half dead." Luke 10:30. "And he said, A certain man had two sons: And the younger of them said to his father, Father, give me the portion of goods that falleth to me. And he divided unto them his living." Luke 15:11, 12.

19. Why did Jesus enter triumphantly into Jerusalem?

A. *In that way He offered Himself as the King of the Jews.*

"Rejoice greatly, O daughter of Zion; shout, O daughter of Jerusalem: behold, thy King cometh unto thee: he is just, and having salvation; lowly, and riding upon an ass, and upon a colt the foal of an ass." Zechariah 9:9.

20. What was the last time that Jesus was alone with His disciples before the Crucifixion?

A. Jesus was alone with His disciples at the feast of unleavened bread which typified the Holy Communion or the Lord's Supper.

"And the disciples did as Jesus had appointed them; and they made ready the passover. And as they were eating, Jesus took bread, and blessed it, and brake it, and gave it to the disciples, and said, Take, eat; this is my body." Matthew 26:19, 26.

21. Why did Jesus go to the Garden of Gethsemane?

A. Jesus went there to pray to His heavenly Father for strength to go through with the crucifixion which He knew would take place within a few hours.

"Then cometh Jesus with them unto a place called Gethsemane, and saith unto the disciples, Sit ye here, while I go and pray yonder." Matthew 26:36.

22. Who betrayed Jesus?

A. *Judas Iscariot betrayed Jesus for thirty pieces of silver.*

"Then one of the twelve, called Judas Iscariot, went unto the chief priests. And said unto them, What will ye give me, and I will deliver him unto you? And they convenanted with him for thirty pieces of silver." Matthew 26:14, 15.

23. Where was Jesus brought to trial?

A. *He was tried before Jewish and Roman courts.*

"And they that had laid hold on Jesus led him away to Caiaphas the high priest, where the scribes and the elders were assembled. And when they had bound him, they led him away, and delivered him to Pontius Pilate the governor." Matthew 26:57; 27:2.

24. What was the charge the Jews brought against Jesus?

A. *They said Jesus was guilty of blasphemy because He said He was the Son of God.*

"Again the high priest asked him, and said unto him, Art thou the Christ, the Son of the Blessed? And Jesus said, I am: and ye shall see the Son of man sitting on the right hand of power, and coming in the clouds of heaven. Then the high priest rent his clothes, and saith, What need we any further witnesses? Ye have heard the blasphemy: what think ye?" Mark 14:61-64.

25. What was the verdict and the sentence?

A. *They condemned Him and delivered Him to be crucified.*

"—And they all condemned him to be guilty of death." Mark 14:64b.

26. Why did God permit them to crucify His Son?

A. God gave His Son to be the Saviour of the world, and to suffer and die in the place of sinful men.

"For God so loved the world, that he gave his only begotten Son, that whosoever believeth in him should not perish, but have everlasting life." John 3:16.

27. How was Jesus buried?

A. *Joseph of Arimathea and Nicodemus buried Him in a new rock-hewn tomb.*

"And after this Joseph of Arimathaea, being a disciple of Jesus, but secretly for fear of the Jews, besought Pilate that he might take away the body of Jesus: and Pilate gave him leave. He came therefore, and took the body of Jesus. And there came also Nicodemus, which at the first came to Jesus by night, and brought a mixture of myrrh and aloes, about an hundred pound weight." John 19:38, 39.

28. How long was Jesus in the grave?

A. Jesus was in the grave for three days and three nights.

"For as Jonas was three days and three nights in the

whale's belly; so shall the Son of man be three days and three nights in the heart of the earth." Matthew 12:40.

29. What happened at the end of this time?

A. Jesus rose from the dead and left an angel at His tomb to announce His resurrection to His sorrowing disciples.

"And, behold, there was a great earthquake: for the angel of the Lord descended from heaven, and came and rolled back the stone from the door, and sat upon it. And the angel answered and said unto the women, He is not here: for he is risen. Come, see the place where the Lord lay." Matthew 28:2, 5, 6.

30. What happened on the fortieth day after the resurrection?

A. Jesus called His disciples out to the Mount of Olives, and while they looked on, He ascended up into heaven.

"And it came to pass, while he blessed them, he was parted from them, and carried up into heaven." Luke 24:51.

31. What did He tell His disciples just before His ascension?

A. He told them to tarry in Jerusalem until He sent the Holy Ghost upon them, and then to go into all the world and preach the gospel to every creature.

"And, behold, I send the promise of my Father upon you: but tarry ye in the city of Jerusalem, until ye be endued with power from on high. And he said unto them, Go ye into all the world, and preach the gospel to every creature." Luke 24:49; *Mark* 16:15.

32. What was the message of the angels to the disciples on that day?

A. They told them that Jesus would come again just as He went away

"Which also said, *Ye men of Galilee, why stand ye gazing up into heaven? this same Jesus, which is taken up from you into heaven, shall so come in like manner as ye have seen him go into heaven." Acts* 1:11.

IX. THE ACTS

1. How many of His disciples returned to Jerusalem to tarry for the Holy Spirit after Jesus' ascension?

A. *There were* 120 *who tarried for the Holy Spirit in Jerusalem.*

"And in those days Peter stood up in the midst of the disciples, and said, (the number of names together were about an hundred and twenty)." Acts 1:15.

2. On what day did the Holy Spirit fall?

A. The Holy Spirit first fell on the Day of Pentecost, which was 50 days after Jesus' resurrection.

"And when the day of Pentecost was fully come, they were all with one accord in one place." Acts 2:1.

3. What were the disciples doing when the Holy Spirit came upon them?

A. They were worshiping God.

"And were continually in the temple, praising and blessing God." Luke 24:53.

4. What was the sign of the coming of the Holy Spirit?

A. *"There came a sound from heaven as of a rushing mighty wind, and it filled all the house where they were sitting. And there appeared unto them cloven tongues like as of fire, and it sat on each of them. And they were all filled with the Holy Ghost, and began to speak with other tongues, as the Spirit gave them utterance." Acts* 2:2-4.

5. What was the coming of the Holy Spirit on the Day of Pentecost the beginning of?

A. *This was the beginning of the dispensation of grace. It was also the beginning of the Christian church.*

"Then they that gladly received his word were baptized: and the same day there were added unto them about three thousand souls. Praising God, and having favour with all the people. And the Lord added to the church daily such as should be saved." Acts 2:41, 47.

6. What happened immediately after the Holy Spirit came on the Day of Pentecost?

A. *The crowds came together and Peter preached to them.*

"Now when this was noised abroad, the multitude came together, and were confounded, because that every man heard them speak in his own language. But Peter standing up with the eleven, lifted up his voice, and said unto them, Ye men of Judea, and all ye that dwell at Jerusalem, be this known unto you, and hearken to my words." Acts 2:6, 14.

7. What were the results of this first gospel service in this dispensation?

A. *Three thousand souls were saved and added to the church.*

"Then they that gladly received his word were baptized: and the same day there were added unto them about three thousand souls." Acts 2:41.

8. What was the first recorded miracle of the early church?

A. *The healing of the lame man at the Beautiful Gate.*

"And a certain man lame from his mother's womb was carried, whom they laid daily at the gate of the temple which is called Beautiful, to ask alms of them that entered into the temple; And he leaping up stood, and walked, and entered with them into the temple, walking and leaping, and praising God." Acts 3:2, 8.

9. What was the effect of this miracle upon the people?

A. *The people wondered greatly and many be-*

lieved, the number of men being about five thousand.

"And they knew that it was he which sat for alms at the Beautiful gate of the temple: and they were filled with wonder and amazement at that which had happened unto him. Howbeit many of them which heard the word believed; and the number of the men was about five thousand." Acts 3:10; 4:4.

10. What happened to the apostles after the first miracle?

A. *The priests were angry at them and put them in prison, but later released them.*

"And they laid hands on them, and put them in hold unto the next day: for it was now eventide. So when they had further theatened them, they let them go, finding nothing how they might punish them, because of the people: for all men glorified God for that which was done." Acts 4:3, 21.

11. What was the attitude of the Church toward sin in those days?

A. *The Church was afraid of sin, for when Ananias and Sapphira told a falsehood about their gifts the Holy Spirit smote them dead.*

"Whiles it remained, was it not thine own? and after it was sold, was it not in thine own power? why hast thou conceived this thing in thine heart? thou hast not lied unto men, but unto God. And Ananias hearing these words fell down, and gave up the ghost: and great fear came on all them that heard these things." Acts 5:4, 5.

12. Were there other miracles performed?

A. *Many signs and wonders were done by the apostles,* so much that the very shadow of Peter falling on sick people resulted in their healing.

"And by the hands of the apostles were many signs and wonders wrought among the people; (and they were all with one accord in Solomon's porch.) Insomuch that they brought forth the sick into the streets, and laid them on beds and couches, that at the least the shadow of Peter passing by might overshadow some of them." Acts 5:12, 15.

13. What effect did the miracles have upon the rulers?

A. *They became angry and put the apostles into jail and beat them.*

"Then the high priest rose up, and all they that were with him, . . . and were filled with indignation. And laid their hands on the apostles, and put them in the common prison." Acts 5:17, 18.

14. Name two of the seven deacons chosen to serve the church who later became strong preachers.

A. *Stephen and Philip.*

"And Stephen, full of faith and power, did great wonders and miracles among the people. Then Philip went down to the city of Samaria, and preached Christ unto them." Acts 6:8; 8:5.

15. For what is Stephen known particularly?

A. *Stephen was the first Christian martyr.*

"And they stoned Stephen, calling upon God, and saying, Lord Jesus, receive my spirit." Acts 7:59.

16. At whose feet did the men who stoned Stephen lay their clothes?

A. *They laid them at the feet of Saul of Tarsus, one of the chief persecutors of the Christians.*

"And cast him out of the city, and stoned him: and the witnesses laid down their clothes at a young man's feet, whose name was Saul." Acts 7:58.

17. What did Philip do?

A. *He became an evangelist and had a great revival at Samaria.*

"Then Philip went down to the city of Samaria, and preached Christ unto them." Acts 8:5.

18. What became of Saul of Tarsus?

A. *He later was converted and became the Apostle Paul.*

"And Saul, yet breathing out threatenings and slaughter

against the disciples of the Lord, went unto the high priest. . . . And he trembling and astonished, said, Lord, what wilt thou have me to do? And the Lord said unto him, Arise, and go into the city, and it shall be told thee what thou must do. And straightway he preached Christ in the synagogues, that he is the Son of God." Acts 9:1, 6, 20.

19. How did Saul become converted?

A. *Jesus appeared to him while he was on his way to Damascus.*

"And he fell to the earth, and heard a voice saying unto him, Saul, Saul, why persecutest thou me? And he said, Who art thou, Lord? And the Lord said, I am Jesus whom thou persecutest: it is hard for thee to kick against the pricks." Acts 9:4, 5.

20. What did Paul do after he was converted?

A. *He preached Christ at Damascus and later with Barnabas became the church's first official misionary.*

"But Saul increased the more in strength, and confounded the Jews which dwelt at Damascus, proving that this is the very Christ." Acts 9:22.

21. Where did Paul go on his first missionary journey?

A. *Paul went to the island of Cyprus, to Antioch in Pisidia, and to Iconium, Lystra, and Derbe.*

"So they, being sent forth by the Holy Ghost, departed unto Seleucia; and from thence they sailed to Cyprus. Now when Paul and his company loosed from Paphos, they came to Perga in Pamphylia: and John departing from them returned to Jerusalem." Acts 13:4, 13. "Howbeit, as the disciples stood round about him, he rose up, and came into the city: and the next day he departed with Barnabas to Derbe." Acts 14:20.

22. Who went with Paul on his second missionary journey?

A. *The prophet Silas went with Paul on his second missionary journey.*

"And Judas and Silas, being prophets also themselves, exhorted the brethren with many words, and confirmed them." Acts 15:32

23. Where did Paul and Silas go on this journey?

A. *They went through Syria and Cilicia and as far as Philippi, Thessalonica, Athens, and Corinth and back to Jerusalem and Antioch.*

"And he went through Syria and Cilicia, confirming the churches." Acts 15:41.

"And when he had landed at Caesarea, and gone up, and saluted the church, he went down to Antioch." Acts 18:22.

24. What happened on Paul's third missionary journey?

A. *He traveled throughout Galatia and Phrygia to Ephesus and back over the same ground he had covered in his second journey.*

"And after he had spent some time there, he departed, and went over all the country of Galatia and Phrygia in order, strengthening all the disciples." Acts 18:23.

25. What happened at the end of Paul's third missionary journey?

A. *He was arrested at Jerusalem and kept in prison at Caesarea for over two years.*

"And all the city was moved, and people ran together: and they took Paul, and drew him out of the temple: and forthwith the doors were shut." Acts 21:30.

"But after two years Porcius Festus came into Felix' room: and Felix, willing to shew the Jews a pleasure, left Paul bound." Acts 24:27.

26. What happened at the end of this imprisonment?

A. *Paul appealed his case to Caesar and was taken to Rome for trial there.*

"For if I be an offender, or have committed any thing worthy of death, I refuse not to die: but if there be none of these things whereof these accuse me, no man may deliver me unto them. I appeal unto Caesar. But when Paul had appealed to be reserved unto the hearing of Augustus, I commanded him to be kept till I might send him to Caesar." Acts 25:11, 21.

27. Did Paul have an easy voyage?

A. *No. His ship was wrecked in a storm, but no one lost his life.*

"Paul stood forth in the midst of them, and said, . . . I exhort you to be of good cheer: for there shall be no loss of any man's life among you, but of the ship. For there stood by me this night the angel of God, whose I am, and whom I serve, saying, Fear not, Paul; thou must be brought before Caesar: and, lo, God hath given thee all them that sail with thee." Acts 27:21-24.

28. What became of Paul?

A. *He was kept in Rome for two years awaiting trial.*

"And Paul dwelt two whole years in his own hired house, and received all that came in unto him." Acts 28:30.

29. What did Paul do when he was in prison?

A. *He wrote letters to the churches which he had founded.*

"For this cause I Paul, the prisoner of Jesus Christ for you Gentiles." Ephesians 3:1.

30. Are Paul's letters in existence today?

A. *Yes. They are among the Epistles of the New Testament.*

PART 2
Bible Doctrine, Christian Living
for Children

A. DOCTRINE

I. The Bible

1. Who wrote the book that is called the Bible?

A. Holy men of God wrote the Bible.

"Holy men of God spake as they were moved by the Holy Ghost." 2 Peter 1:21.

2. Of what does the Bible consist?

A. *The Bible consists of the Old Testament of 39 books and the New Testament of 27 books. It is thus a library of 66 books.*

3. How is the Bible different from all other books?

A. It is the only book in the world that is wholly inspired by God.

"All scripture is given by inspiration of God, and is profitable for doctrine, for reproof, for correction, for instruction in righteousness." 2 Timothy 3:16.

4. Why did God give us the Bible?

A. *God gave us the Bible to show us the way of salvation and to teach us how to live for Him.*

"Thy Word is a lamp unto my feet and a light unto my path." "Thy Word have I hid in mine heart that I might not sin against thee." Psalm 119:105, 11.

II. God

1. What is God?

A. *God is a Spirit.*

"God is a spirit: and they that worship Him must worship Him in spirit and in truth." John 4:24

2. How many gods are there?

A. *There is only one true God.*

"Hear, O Israel: The Lord, our God, is one Lord." Deuteronomy 6:4.

3. How many Persons are in the Godhead?

A. *There are three Persons in the Godhead: Father, Son, and Holy Ghost.*

"Go ye therefore, and teach all nations, baptizing them in the name of the Father, and of the Son, and of the Holy Ghost." Matthew 28:19.

"For there are three that bear record in heaven, the Father, the Word, and the Holy Ghost, and these three are one." 1 John 5:7.

4. Name some of the qualities of God.

A. *God is good, holy, just, all-powerful, all-knowing and eternal.*

"And the Lord passed by before him, and proclaimed, *The Lord, The Lord God, merciful and gracious, longsuffering, and abundant in goodness and truth."* Exodus 34:6.

"For I am the Lord your God: ye shall therefore sanctify yourselves, and ye shall be holy; for I am holy: neither shall ye defile yourselves with any manner of creeping thing that creepeth upon the earth." Leviticus 11:44.

"And all the inhabitants of the earth are reputed as nothing: and he doeth according to his will in the army of heaven, and among the inhabitants of the earth: and none can stay his hand, or say unto him, What doest thou?" Daniel 4:35.

"Neither is there any creature that is not manifest in his sight: but all things are naked and opened unto the eyes of him with whom we have to do." Hebrews 4:13.

"And sware by him that liveth for ever and ever, who created heaven, and the things that therein are, and the earth, and the things that therein are, and the sea, and the things which are therein, that there should be time no longer." Revelation 10:6.

5. What should be our attitude toward God?

"Thou shalt love the Lord thy God with all thy heart,

A. *We should love God above all others.*
and with all thy soul, and with all thy mind." Matthew 22:37.

III. MAN

1. How did God make man?

A. God formed man from the dust of the ground and breathed upon him to give him life.

"The Lord God formed man of the dust of the ground, and breathed into his nostrils the breath of life; and man became a living soul." Genesis 2:7.

"God said, Let us make man in our image, after our likeness; and let them have dominion over the fish of the sea, and over the fowl of the air, and over the cattle, and over all the earth, and over every creeping thing that creepeth upon the earth. So God created man in His own image, in the image of God created He him; male and female created He them." Genesis 1:26, 27.

2. Why did God make man?

A. *God made man that he might glorify God.*
"That we should be to the praise of his glory." Ephesians 1:12.

3. What was man's condition when first created?

A. *He was perfect in body, soul and spirit.*

4. Did man remain in this perfect state?

A. *No.   He disobeyed God and thus fell from his perfect state.*

"For as by one man's disobedience many were made sinners, so by the obedience of one shall many be made righteous." Romans 5:19.

IV. SIN

1. What is sin?

A. *Sin is disobeying the commandments of God.*
"Sin is the transgression of the law." 1 John 3:4.

2. Who brought sin into the world?

A. *Satan tempted man to sin and man yielded to that temptation.*
"He that committeth sin is of the devil; for the devil sinneth from the beginnning." 1 John 3:8.

3. If Satan tempted man to sin, was man to blame for his sin?

A. *Yes, for he did not have to yield to the temptation.*

"Let no man say when he is tempted, I am tempted of God: for God cannot be tempted with evil, neither tempteth he any man: but every man is tempted, when he is drawn away of his own lust, and enticed." James 1:13, 14.

4. What happened to man when he sinned?

A. *Death began to work immediately in his spirit, soul and body.*

"Wherefore, as by one man sin entered into the world, and death by sin; and so death passed upon all men, for that all have sinned." Romans 5:12.

5. Is sin in the world today?

A. *Yes. All people are sinners.*

"For all have sinned, and come short of the glory of God." Romans 3:23.

6. What is the penalty of sin?

A. *The penalty of sin is death and everlasting punishment.*

"Death passed upon all men, for that all have sinned." Romans 5:12.

"The wages of sin is death." Romans 6:23.

7. How can we escape the penalty of sin?

A. *We can escape the penalty of sin only by accepting Christ.*

"God commendeth his love toward us, in that, while we were yet sinners, Christ died for us." Romans 5:8.

"And she shall bring forth a son, and thou shalt call his name JESUS: for he shall save his people from their sins." Matthew 1:21.

V. JESUS CHRIST

1. Who is Jesus Christ?

A. Jesus Christ is the only begotten Son of God and also the Son of Man, being born of the Virgin Mary.

"And the angel said unto her, Fear not, Mary: for thou hast found favor with God. And, behold, thou shalt . . . bring forth a son, and shalt call his name JESUS. He shall be great, and shall be called the Son of the Highest: and the Lord God shall give unto him the throne of his father David. He shall reign over the house of Jacob for ever; and of His kingdom there shall be no end." Luke 1:30-33.

"And the Word was made flesh, and dwelt among us, (and we beheld his glory, the glory as of the only begotten of the Father,) full of grace and truth." John 1:14.

2. What does the word "Jesus" mean?

A. *It means "Saviour."*

"And she shall bring forth a son, and thou shalt call his name JESUS: for he shall save his people from their sins." Matthew 1:21.

3. What does the word "Christ" mean?

A. It means "The Anointed One," or "The Messiah."

"And Simon Peter answered and said, Thou art the Christ, the Son of the living God." Matthew 16:16.

4. Who is Jesus' Father?

A. *God is Jesus' Father.*

"Jesus Christ . . . received from God the Father honor and glory, when there came such a voice to him from the excellent glory, *This is my beloved Son, in whom I am well pleased.*" 2 Peter 1:17.

"*And Simon Peter answered and said, Thou art the Christ, the Son of the living God.*" Matthew 16:16.

5. Who was Jesus' mother?

A. *Mary was the mother of Jesus.*

"*And the angel said unto her, Fear not, Mary: for thou hast found favor with God. Behold, thou shalt . . . bring forth a son, and shalt call his name Jesus.*" Luke 1:30, 31.

6. Does this make Jesus human?

A. *Yes. Jesus is both human and divine,* (two natures in one Person.)

"*Concerning his Son Jesus Christ our Lord, which was made of the seed of David according to the flesh; and declared to be the Son of God with power, according to the spirit of holiness, by the resurrection from the dead.*" Romans 1:3, 4.

7. Why did Jesus come into the world?

A. *Jesus came into the world to save man from sin.*

"*For the Son of man is come to seek and to save that which was lost.' Luke 19:10.*

"The Son of man came not to be ministered unto, but to minister, and to give his life a ransom for many." Matthew 20:28.

8. How did Jesus save man from sin?

A. *Jesus died on the cross of Calvary to save man from his sin.*

"The blood of Jesus Christ his Son cleanseth us from all sin." 1 John 1:7.

"Ye know that ye were not redeemed with corruptible things, as silver and gold, . . . but with the precious blood of Christ, as of a lamb without blemish and without spot." 1 Peter 1:18, 19.

9. Then are all men now saved since Jesus died for them?

A. *Each man has to accept Jesus as his personal Saviour, otherwise Jesus' death will not save him.*

"And he said unto them, Go ye into all the world, and preach the gospel to every creature. *He that believeth and is baptized shall be saved; but he that believeth not shall be damned.*" Mark 16:15, 16.

"For God so loved the world, that he gave his only begotten Son, that whosoever believeth in him should not perish, but have everlasting life. For God sent not his Son into the world to condemn the world; but that the world through him might be saved. He that believeth on him is not condemned: but he that believeth not is condemned already, because he hath not believed in the name of the only begotten Son of God." John 3:16-18.

"He that believeth on the Son hath everlasting life: and he that believeth not the Son shall not see life; but the wrath of God abideth on him." John 3:36.

10. What miraculous thing happened three days after Jesus' crucifixion?

A. *Jesus rose from the dead and was seen many times by His disciples.*

"And that he was buried, and that he rose again the third day according to the scriptures: and that he was seen of Cephas, then of the twelve: after that, he was seen of above five hundred brethren at once; of whom the greater part remain unto this present, but some are fallen asleep. After that, he was seen of James; then of all the apostles." 1 Corinthians 15:4-7.

11. What does Jesus' resurrection prove?

A. Jesus' resurrection proves that He is the Son of God.

" (Jesus Christ was) declared to be the Son of God with power, according to the spirit of holiness, by the resurrection from the dead." Romans 1:4.

12. What finally became of Jesus?

A. *He ascended up to heaven while His disciples were watching.*

"And he led them out as far as to Bethany, and he lifted up his hands, and blessed them. *And it came to pass, while he blessed them, he was parted from them, and carried up into heaven." Luke* 24:50, 51.

13. What is Jesus doing now?

A. *Jesus is seated at the right hand of the Father making intercession for us.*

"If any man sin, we have an Advocate with the Father, Jesus Christ the Righteous." 1 John 2:1.
"Wherefore he is able also to save them to the uttermost that come unto God by him, seeing he ever liveth to make intercession for them." Hebrews 7:25.

14. Will Jesus come back to this earth again?

A. *Yes. Jesus will come again just as He went away.*

"This same Jesus, which is taken up from you into heaven, shall so come in like manner as ye have seen him go into heaven." Acts 1:11.

"For the Lord himself shall descend from heaven with a shout, with the voice of the archangel, and with the trump of God: and the dead in Christ shall rise first: then we which are alive and remain shall be caught up together with them in the clouds to meet the Lord in the air: and so shall we ever be with the Lord." 1 Thessalonians 4:16, 17.

VI. SALVATION

1. What is meant by salvation?

A. *Salvation means to be set free from sin and its penalty.*

"Unto him that loved us, and washed us from our sins in his own blood." Revelation 1:5.

"Much more then, being now justified by his blood, we shall be saved from wrath through him." Romans 5:9.

2. Why must we be saved?

A. *We must be saved because we are all lost in sin and on our way to hell.*

"For all have sinned, and come short of the glory of God." Romans 3:23.

"The soul that sinneth, it shall die." Ezekiel 18:4.

3. What must we do to be saved?

A. We must believe on the Lord Jesus Christ in order to be saved.

"Believe on the Lord Jesus Christ, and thou shalt be saved." Acts 16:31.

"If thou shalt confess with thy mouth the Lord Jesus, and shalt believe in thine heart that God hath raised him from the dead, thou shalt be saved. For with the heart man believeth unto righteousness, and with the mouth confession is made unto salvation." Romans 10:9, 10.

4. What must we do about our sins?

A. We must repent of our sins and ask God for Christ's sake to forgive us and cleanse our hearts from all sin.

"If we confess our sins, he is faithful and just to forgive us our sins, and to cleanse us from all unrighteousness." 1 John 1:9.

"Godly sorrow worketh repentance to salvation." 2 Corinthians 7:10.

5. What happens to us when we become saved?

A. *We are born into the family of God by the Holy Spirit.* This is what Jesus meant when he said: "Ye must be born again."

"Jesus answered and said unto him, Verily, verily, I say unto thee, Except a man be born again, he cannot see the kingdom of God." John 3:3.

"If any man be in Christ, he is a new creature: old things are passed away; behold, all things are become new." 2 Corinthians 5:17.

6. What does justification mean?

A. *Justification means that God declares one to be free from guilt ("just as if" he had not sinned) and declares him to be righteous in His sight.*

"Therefore being justified by faith, we have peace with God through our Lord Jesus Christ." Romans 5:1.

7. What is adoption?

A. *It is an act of God whereby a sinner is forgiven and actually adopted into the family of God and counted as a son entitled to full inheritance.*

"The Spirit itself beareth witness with our spirit, that we are the children of God: and if children, then heirs; heirs of God, and joint-heirs with Christ; if so be that we suffer with him, that we may be also glorified together." Romans 8:16-17.

8. How can one know that he is saved?

A. *One can know that he is saved by believing God's Word, by having the witness of the Spirit in his heart and by loving the brethren.*

"The Spirit itself beareth witness with our spirit, that we are the children of God." Romans 8:16.

"And this is his commandment, That we should believe on the name of his Son Jesus Christ, and love one another, as he gave us commandment." 1 John 3:23.

9. What is meant by sanctification?

A. *Sanctification means being cleansed from sin and dedicated to God.*

"And the very God of peace sanctify you wholly; and I pray God your whole spirit and soul and body be preserved blameless unto the coming of our Lord Jesus Christ." 1 Thessalonians 5:23.

10. Is it God's will that all Christians should be sanctified?

A. *Yes. Our sanctification is the will of God, and without holiness no man shall see the Lord.*

"For this is the will of God even your sanctification, that ye should abstain from fornication." 1 Thessalonians 4:3.

"Follow peace with all men, and holiness, without which no man shall see the Lord." Hebrews 12:14.

11. What is divine healing?

A. *It is the supernatural power of God working healing in the human body.*

"Is any sick among you? Let him call for the elders of the church; and let them pray over him, anointing him with oil in the name of the Lord: and the prayer of faith shall save the sick, and the Lord shall raise him up; and if he have committed sins, they shall be forgiven him." James 5:14, 15.

12. Was this blessing of divine healing included in the benefits which Jesus purchased for us on Calvary?

A. *Yes. Divine healing was included in the benefits Jesus purchased for us on Calvary.*

"They brought unto him many that were possessed with devils; *and he cast out the spirits with his word, and healed all that were sick: that it might be fulfillled which was spoken by Esaias the prophet, saying, Himself took our infirmities, and bare our sicknesses.*" *Matthew* 8:16, 17.

13. Of what does worship consist?

A. *Worship consists of prayer, praise and adoration.*

"And as they went to tell his disciples, behold, Jesus met them, saying, All hail. And they came and held him by the feet, and worshipped him." Matthew 28:9.

14. How often should Christians give thanks?

A. Christians are commanded to give thanks always in all things and for all things.

"Giving thanks always for all things unto God and the Father in the name of our Lord Jesus Christ." Ephesians 5:20.

"*In everything give thanks: for this is the will of God in Christ Jesus concerning you.*" *1 Thessalonians* 5:18.

15. How important is prayer to a Christian?

A. *Prayer is the very breath of true Christian living.*

"Rejoicing in hope; patient in tribulation; continuing instant in prayer." Romans 12:12.

16. What is the power of faith?

A. *Faith brings salvation, healing, the Baptism in the Holy Spirit, and all of God's blessings.* Without faith it is impossible to please God.

"*Jesus said unto him, If thou canst believe, all things are possible to him that believeth.*" *Mark* 9:23.

"*But without faith it is impossible to please him:* for he that cometh to God must believe that he is, and that he is a rewarder of them that diligently seek him." Hebrews 11:6.

"That the blessing of Abraham might come on the Gentiles through Jesus Christ; that we might receive the promise of the Spirit through faith." Galatians 3:14.

"And the prayer of faith shall save the sick, and the Lord shall raise him up; and if he have committed sins, they shall be forgiven him." James 5:15.

"For by grace are ye saved through faith; and that not of yourselves: it is the gift of God." Ephesians 2:8.

17. What is the greatest of Christian virtues?

A. *Love is the greatest Christian virtue.* It is the real measure of spirituality.

"And now abideth faith, hope, charity, these three; but the greatest of these is charity." 1 Corinthians 13:13.

18. Whom should Christians love?

A. *Christians should love God, Christ, each other, lost men, and even their enemies.*

"Jesus said unto him, Thou shalt love the Lord thy God with all thy heart, and with all thy soul, and with all thy mind." Matthew 22:37.

"A new commandment I give unto you, That ye love one another; as I have loved you, that ye also love one another." John 13:34.

"But I say unto you, Love your enemies, bless them that curse you, do good to them that hate you, and pray for them which despitefully use you, and persecute you." Matthew 5:44.

VII. THE HOLY SPIRIT

1. Who is the Holy Spirit?

A. *The Holy Spirit is* God. He is *the third Person in the Godhead,* or in the Holy Trinity.

"Go ye therefore, and teach all nations, baptizing them in the name of the Father, and of the Son, and of the Holy Ghost." Matthew 28:19.

Note: The Holy Spirit is also called the Holy Ghost, the Spirit of God, the Spirit of Christ, and the Comforter.

2. How does the Holy Spirit show that He is God?

A. *The Holy Spirit shows that He is God because He is like God in every way.*

"*The Spirit searcheth all things, yea, the deep things of God.*" 1 Corinthians 2:10.

"Whither shall I go from Thy Spirit? or whither shall I flee from thy presence? If I ascend up into heaven, Thou art there: if I make my bed in hell, behold, Thou art there. If I take the wings of the morning, and dwell in the uttermost parts of the sea; even there shall Thy hand lead me, and Thy right hand shall hold me." Psalm 139:7-10.

3. Did the Holy Spirit have a part in the creation of the world?

A. *Yes.* The Holy Spirit was active in the creation.

"*And the earth was without form, and void; and darkness was upon the face of the deep. And the Spirit of God moved on the face of the waters. And God said, Let there be light: and there was light.*" Genesis 1:2, 3.

"The Spirit of God hath made me, and the breath of the Almighty hath given me life." Job 33:4.

4. Was the Holy Spirit present in Old Testament time?

A. *The Holy Spirit has existed from all eternity.*

"*How much more shall the blood of Christ, who through the eternal Spirit offered himself without spot to God, purge your conscience from dead works to serve the living God?*" Hebrews 9:14.

"My Spirit will not always strive with man." Genesis 6:3.

"And Pharaoh said unto his servants, Can we find such a one as this is, a man in whom the Spirit of God is?" Genesis 41:38.

5. What part does the Holy Spirit have in conversion?

A. *The Holy Spirit is the One who convicts of sin and produces conversion.*

"And when He (the Holy Spirit) is come, He will reprove the world of sin, and of righteousness, and of judgment." John 16:8.

"No man can say that Jesus is the Lord, but by the Holy Ghost." 1 Corinthians 12:3.

"Jesus answered, Verily, verily, I say unto thee, Except a man be born of water and of the Spirit, he cannot enter into the kingdom of God. That which is born of the flesh is flesh; and that which is born of the Spirit is spirit." John 3:5, 6.

6. Does the Holy Spirit dwell in every believer?

A. *Yes. The Holy Spirit comes into one's heart when he is converted.*

"God hath sent forth the Spirit of His Son into your hearts, crying, Abba, Father." Galatians 4:6.

"If any man have not the Spirit of Christ, he is none of his." Romans 8:9.

"For ye have not received the spirit of bondage again to fear; but ye have received the Spirit of adoption, whereby we cry, Abba, Father. The Spirit itself beareth witness with our spirit, that we are the children of God." Romans 8:15, 16.

7. Is every believer baptized in the Holy Spirit?

A. *No. But Christians today may and should be baptized into the Holy Spirit after they are converted.*

"Then Peter said unto them, Repent, and be baptized every one of you in the name of Jesus Christ for the remission of sins, and ye shall receive the gift of the Holy Ghost. For the promise is unto you, and to your children, and to all that are afar off, even as many as the Lord our God shall call." Acts 2:38, 39.

VIII. THE CHURCH

1. What is the Church?

A. *The Church is the Body of Christ of which He is the Head.*

"Now ye are the body of Christ, and members in particular." 1 Corinthians 12:27.

2. What else does the Bible call the Church?

A. *The Bible calls the Church the Bride.*

"Husbands, love your wives, even as Christ also loved

the Church, and gave himself for it; that he might sanctify and cleanse it with the washing of water by the word, that he might present it to himself a glorious church, not having spot, or wrinkle, or any such thing; but that it should be holy and without blemish. So ought men to love their wives as their own bodies. He that loveth his wife loveth himself. For no man ever yet hated his own flesh; but nourisheth and cherisheth it, even as the Lord the church. For we are members of his body, of his flesh, and of his bones. For this cause shall a man leave his father and mother, and shall be joined unto his wife, and they two shall be one flesh." Ephesians 5:25-32.

The Bible calls the Church a Temple.

"In whom all the building fitly framed together groweth unto an holy temple in the Lord." Ephesians 2:21.

The Bible calls the Church a Vine.

"I am the true vine, and my Father is the husbandman. Every branch in me that beareth not fruit he taketh away; and every branch that beareth fruit, he purgeth it, that it may bring forth more fruit. Now ye are clean through the word which I have spoken unto you. Abide in me, and I in you. As the branch cannot bear fruit of itself, except it abide in the vine; no more can ye, except ye abide in me. *I am the vine, ye are the branches. He that abideth in me, and I in him, the same bringeth forth much fruit: for without me ye can do nothing.* If a man abide not in me, he is cast forth as a branch, and is withered; and men gather them, and cast them into the fire, and they are burned. If ye abide in me, and my words abide in you, ye shall ask what ye will, and it shall be done unto you. Herein is my Father glorified, that ye bear much fruit; so shall ye be my disciples." John 15:1-8.

3. Of whom does the Church consist?

A. *The Church consists of all those who are truly born-again followers of Christ.*

"For ye are all the children of God by faith in Christ Jesus. For as many of you as have been baptized into Christ have put on Christ. *There is neither Jew nor*

Greek, there is neither bond nor free, there is neither male nor female: for ye are all one in Christ Jesus. And if ye be Christ's, then are ye Abraham's seed, and heirs according to the promise." Galatians 3:26-29.

4. What are the ordinances of the Church?

A. *The ordinances of the Church are water baptism and holy communion.*

"Go ye therefore, and teach all nations, baptizing them in the name of the Father, and of the Son, and of the Holy Ghost." Matthew 28:19.

"For I have received of the Lord that which also I delivered unto you, that the Lord Jesus the same night in which he was betrayed took bread; and when he had given thanks, he brake it, and said, Take, eat: this is my body, which is broken for you: this do in remembrance of me. After the same manner also he took the cup, when he had supped, saying, This cup is the new testament in my blood: this do ye, as oft as ye drink it, in remembrance of me. For as often as ye eat this bread, and drink this cup, ye do shew the Lord's death till he come." 1 Corinthians 11:23-26.

5. What is the mission of the Church?

A. *The mission of the Church is to preach the gospel to every creature.*

"Thus it is written, and thus it behoved Christ to suffer, and to rise from the dead the third day: and that repentance and remission of sins should be preached in his name among all nations." Luke 24:46, 47.

"And he (Jesus) said unto them, Go ye into all the world, and preach the gospel to every creature." Mark 16:15.

6. What is the destiny of the Church?

A. *The final destiny of the Church is to be with Christ throughout eternity.*

"Christ also loved the church, and gave himself for it; that he might sanctify and cleanse it with the washing of water by the Word, that he might present it to himself a glorious church, not having spot, or wrinkle, or any such thing; but that it should be holy and without blemish." Ephesians 5:25-27

IX. THE SPIRIT WORLD

1. What are angels?

A. *Angels are invisible creatures created by God*

"Are they not all ministering spirits, sent forth to minister for them who shall be heirs of salvation?" Hebrews 1:14.

2. Are there good and bad angels?

A. *Yes. There are good and bad angels. The good angels worship and serve God, but the bad angels worship and serve Satan.*

"When the Son of man shall come in his glory, and all the holy angels with him, then shall he sit upon the throne of his glory." Matthew 25:31.

"But to which of the angels said he at any time, Sit on my right hand, until I make thine enemies thy footstool? Are they not all ministering spirits, sent forth to minister for them who shall be heirs of salvation?" Hebrews 1:13-14.

God spared not the angels that sinned, but cast them down to hell, and delivered them into chains of darkness, to be reserved unto judgment." 2 Peter 2:4.

3. Who is Satan?

A. *Satan is a wicked angel that was cast out of heaven because he wanted to exalt himself above God.*

"How art thou fallen from heaven, O Lucifer, (or Satan). . . . For thou hast said in thine heart, I will ascend into heaven, I will exalt my throne above the stars of God." Isaiah 14:12, 13.

"He (Jesus) said unto them, I beheld Satan as lightning fall from heaven." Luke 10:18.

4. What will become of Satan and the bad angels?

A. *Satan (the devil) and all the bad angels will be cast into hell.*

"And the devil that deceived them was cast into the lake of fire and brimstone, where the beast and the false prophet are, and shall be tormented day and night for ever and ever." Revelation 20:10.

X. PROPHECY

1. Name some of the things Jesus said would happen just before His return.

A. Jesus said that at the time of His return there will be an increase in worldliness and wickedness. False Christs and false prophets will rise up; there will be great earthquakes, famines, pestilences. There will be wars and rumors of wars. The Jews will return to Palestine. These signs are spoken of in Matthew 24 and Luke 21.

2. Do we know exactly when the Lord is coming?

A. No. We cannot know exactly when the Lord is coming.

"Of that day and hour knoweth no man, no, not the angels of heaven, but my Father only." Matthew 24:36.

3. What will happen to Christians when Jesus comes?

A. Those who have died in Christ will be resurrected and those who are alive will be changed. All will be caught up together to meet the Lord in the air.

"Behold, I show you a mystery; we shall not all sleep, but we shall all be changed, in a moment, in the twinkling of an eye, at the last trump: for the trumpet shall sound, and the dead shall be raised incorruptible, and we shall be changed. For this corruptible must put on incorruption, and this mortal must put on immortality." 1 Corinthians 15:51, 52, 53.

"But I would not have you to be ignorant, brethren, conerning them which are asleep, that ye sorrow not, even as others which have no hope. For this we say unto you by the word of the Lord, that we which are alive and remain unto the coming of the Lord shall not prevent them which are asleep. *For the Lord himself shall descend from heaven with a shout, with the voice of the archangel, and with the trump of God: and the dead in Christ shall rise first: then we which are alive and remain shall be caught up together with them in the clouds, to meet the Lord in the air: and so shall we ever be with the Lord."* 1 *Thessalonians* 4:13, 15, 16, 17.

4. Where will Christians go when they are caught up to meet Jesus and their loved ones?

A. *Christians will then go to the judgment seat of Christ and to the marriage supper of the Lamb.*

"For we must all appear before the judgment seat of Christ, that every one may receive the things done in his body, according to that he hath done, whether it be good or bad." 2 *Corinthians* 5:10.

"Let us be glad and rejoice, and give honor to him; for the marriage of the Lamb is come, and his wife hath made herself ready. And to her was granted that she should be arrayed in fine linen, clean and white: for the fine linen is the righteousness of saints. And he saith unto me, Write, *Blessed are they which are called unto the marriage supper of the Lamb."* *Revelation* 19:7-9.

5. Will Jesus come back to this earth to reign?

A. *Jesus will return with His own to reign on the earth a thousand years.*

"Behold, the Lord cometh with ten thousands of his saints." Jude 14.

"Blessed and holy is he that hath part in the first resurrection; on such the second death hath no power, but they shall be priests of God and of Christ, and shall reign with him a thousand years." *Revelation* 20:6.

6. What will happen after this thousand years?

A. *Satan will be loosed again in the earth for a little while. The wicked dead will then be raised to stand before God in judgment, then Satan and his angels, and all the wicked will be cast into hell.*

"And I saw a great white throne, and him that sat on it, from whose face the earth and the heaven fled away; and there was found no place for them. And I saw the dead, small and great, stand before God; and the books were opened: and another book was opened, which is the book of life: and the dead were judged out of those things which were written in the books, according to their works. And the sea gave up the dead which were in it; and death and hell delivered up the dead which were in them: and they were judged every man according to their works. And death and hell were cast into the lake of fire. This is the second death. And whosoever was not found written in the book of life was cast into the lake of fire." Revelation 20:11-15.

7. What happens after the Great White Throne Judgment mentioned above?

A. *The eternal state begins.*

"And I John saw the holy city, new Jerusalem, coming down from God out of heaven, prepared as a bride adorned for her husband. And I heard a great voice out of heaven saying, *Behold, the tabernacle of God is with men, and he will dwell with them, and they shall be his people, and God himself shall be with them, and be their God. And God shall wipe away all tears from their eyes; and there shall be no more death, neither sorrow, nor crying, neither shall there be any more pain; for the former things are passed away."* Revelation 21:2-4.

B. CHRISTIAN LIVING

I. The Law of God

1. Name the Ten Commandments

A. *The Ten Commandments are:*

(1) *Thou shalt have no other gods before me.*

(2) *Thou shalt not make unto thee any graven image.*

(3) *Thou shalt not take the name of the Lord thy God in vain; for the Lord will not hold him guiltless that taketh his name in vain.*

(4) *Remember the sabbath day to keep it holy.*

(5) *Honour thy father and thy mother: that thy days may be long upon the land which the Lord thy God giveth thee.*

(6) *Thou shalt not kill.*

(7) *Thou shalt not commit adultery.*

(8) *Thou shalt not steal.*

(9) *Thou shalt not bear false witness against thy neighbor.*

(10) *Thou shalt not covet.*—Exodus 20.

2. What does the First Commandment mean?

A. *It means we should worship no other things
or person and love God above all others.*
"Then saith Jesus unto him, Get thee hence, Satan: for
it is written, *Thou shalt worship the Lord thy God,
and him only shalt thou serve.*" Matthew 4:10.
"Jesus said unto him, Thou shalt love the Lord thy
God with all thy heart, and with all thy soul, and with
all thy mind." Matthew 22:37.

3. What does the Second Commandment forbid?

A. *It forbids making any image to be worshiped.*
"*Thou shalt not make unto thee any graven image, or
any likeness of any thing that is in heaven above, or
that is in the earth beneath, or that is in the water
under the earth.*" Exodus 20:4.

4. How do people break the Third Commandment?

A. *People break the Third Commandment by
cursing and using vile oaths which include the
name of God or Christ.*
"*Let no corrupt communication proceed out of your
mouth,* but that which is good to the use of edifying,
that it may minister grace unto the hearers." Ephesians
4:29.

**5. What is meant by the commandment to keep the
Sabbath holy?**

A. *The Ten Commandments were given origi-
nally to the Jews who observe the seventh day
as a sabbath day of rest. Christians of the
church age are released from the observance
of the Jewish Sabbath but observe Sunday,
the first day of the week as a day of worship.*
"*One man esteemeth one day above another: another
esteemeth every day alike. Let every man be fully persuaded in his own mind.*" Romans 14:5.
"*Let no man therefore judge you in meat, or in drink,
or in respect of an holyday, or of the new moon, or
of the sabbath days.*" Colossians 2:16.
"*Upon the first day of the week let every one of you
lay by him in store, as God hath prospered him, that*

there be no gatherings when I come." 1 Corinthians 16:2.

"And upon the first day of the week, when the disciples came together to break bread, Paul preached unto them, ready to depart on the morrow; and continued his speech until midnight." Acts 20:7.

6. Does the New Testament teach us to obey our parents?

A. *Yes. Children should obey their parents in the Lord.*

"Children, obey your parents in the Lord: for this is right." Ephesians 6:1.

7. Why is it especially wrong to commit murder?

A. *It is especially wrong to commit murder because man is made in the image of God.*

"Whoso sheddeth man's blood, by man shall his blood be shed: for in the image of God made he man." Genesis 9:6.

8. Is taking human life as an officer of the law or a soldier breaking the commandment not to kill?

A. *No, for God commands us to be obedient to our government even to taking human life.*

"Whoso sheddeth man's blood, by man shall his blood be shed: for in the image of God made he man." Genesis 9:6.

"Let every soul be subject unto the higher powers. For there is no power but of God: the powers that be are ordained of God. . . . For he is the minister of God to thee for good. But if thou do that which is evil, be afraid; for he beareth not the sword in vain: for he is the minister of God, a revenger to execute wrath upon him that doeth evil." Romans 13:1, 4.

9. What is adultery?

A. *Adultery is the sin of breaking the marriage vow.*

"And he saith unto them, Whosoever shall put away his wife and marry another committeth adultery against her." Mark 10:11.

10. Does the New Testament also forbid stealing?

A. *Yes.*

"Let him that stole steal no more; but rather let him

labor, working with his hands the thing which is good, that he may have to give to him that needeth." Ephesians 4:28.

"Exhort servants to be obedient unto their own masters, and to please them well in all things; not answering again; not purloining (stealing), but shewing all good fidelity; that they may adorn the doctrine of God our Saviour in all things." Titus 2:9, 10.

11. What does the Ninth Commandment include?

A. *It includes all lying in word or deed.*

"He that worketh deceit shall not dwell within my house: he that telleth lies shall not tarry in my sight." Psalm 101:7.

"And all liars, shall have their part in the lake which burneth with fire and brimstone: which is the second death." Revelation 21:8b.

12. What does covet mean?

A. *Covet means to greatly desire material things.*
"And he said unto them, take heed, and beware of covetousness: for a man's life consisteth not in the abundance of the things which he possesseth." Luke 12:15.

13. Will the sin of covetousness keep a person out of heaven?

A. *Unless repented of and forsaken, it will keep anyone out of heaven.*

"But fornication, and all uncleanness, or covetousness, let it not be once named among you, as becometh saints." Ephesians 5:3.

14. What are these Ten Commandments called?

A. *The Ten Commandments are the Law of God.*

"Owe no man anything, but to love one another: for he that loveth another hath fulfilled the law. For this, Thou shalt not commit adultery, Thou shall not kill, Thou shalt not steal, Thou shalt not bear false witness, Thou shalt not covet; and if there be any other commandment, it is briefly comprehended in this saying, namely, *Thou shalt love thy neighbor as thyself.*

Love worketh no ill to his neighbor: therefore love is the fulfilling of the law." Romans 13:8-10.

15. What is the purpose of God's law?

A. *The purpose of God's Law is to teach us right from wrong.*

"Wherefore then serveth the law? It was added because of transgressions, till the seed should come to whom the promise was made; and it was ordained by angels in the hand of a mediator. . . . Wherefore the law was our schoolmaster to bring us unto Christ, that we might be justified by faith." Galatians 3: 19, 24.

"For by the law is the knowledge of sin." Romans 3:20.

16. Are Christians today required to keep these Commandments?

A. *Yes, for they all are repeated in the New Testament, except the Fourth Commandment.*

"By this we know that we love the children of God, when we love God, and keep his commandments." 1 John 5:2.

17. Does obedience to God's Law save us?

A. *No. We are saved only by grace through faith in Jesus Christ.*

"For by grace are ye saved through faith; and that not of yourselves: it is the gift of God: Not of works, lest any man should boast." Ephesians 2:8, 9.

18. Why then should we obey the Law?

A. *We should obey God's Law not in order to be saved, but because we are saved and desire above all else to please God.*

"For we are his workmanship, created in Christ Jesus unto good works, which God hath before ordained that we should walk in them." Ephesians 2:10.

19. How can we obey God's Law?

A. *We can obey God's law only by the grace and power of Jesus Christ.*

"For the law of the Spirit of life in Christ Jesus hath made me free from the law of sin and death. For

what the law could not do, that it was weak through the flesh, God sending his own Son in the likeness of sinful flesh, and for sin, condemned sin in the flesh: That the righteousness of the law might be fulfilled in us, who walk not after the flesh, but after the Spirit." Romans 8:2-4.

20. What should we do if we break one of God's commandments?

A. *We should immediately ask God for Christ's sake to forgive us and cleanse us from sin.*

"My little children, these things write I unto you, that ye sin not. And if any man sin, we have an advocate with the Father, Jesus Christ the righteous: And he is the propitiation for our sins: and not for ours only, but also for the sins of the whole world." 1 John 2:1, 2.

II. A Christian's Relationship to God:

1. How is God related to Christians?

A. *God is their heavenly Father, and they are His children.*

"Our Father which art in heaven, Hallowed be thy name." Matthew 6:9.
"Let your light so shine before men, that they may see your good works, and glorify your Father which is in heaven." Matthew 5:16.

2. Is God the Father of everyone?

A. *No. God is the creator of everyone, but He is the Father only of those who have been born into His family.*

"In this the children of God are manifest, and the children of the devil: *whosoever doeth not righteousness is not of God, neither he that loveth not his brother."* 1 John 3:10 Cf John 8:44.

3. How do we become God's children?

A. *We become God's children by accepting Jesus Christ, God's only begotten son, our Saviour.*

"Jesus said unto him, I am the way, the truth, and the

life; no man cometh unto the Father, but by me."
John 14:6.

*"But as many as received him (Jesus), to them gave
he power to become the sons of God, even to them that
believe on his name." John 1:12.*

4. Does the heavenly Father provide for His children?

A. *Yes, He supplies their every need.*

*"My God shall supply all your need according to his
riches in glory by Christ Jesus." Phil. 4:19.*

5. Does the heavenly Father watch over his children?

A. *Yes, He watches over them day and night.*

*"He will not suffer thy foot to be moved: he that keep-
eth thee will not slumber." Psalm 121:3.*

"The eyes of the Lord are upon the righteous, and his
ears are open unto their cry." Psalm 34:15.

6. How may Christians receive blessings from God?

A. *Christians may receive all of God's promises
and blessings through prayer and believing
His Word.*

*"Whatever ye shall ask in my name, that will I do,
that the Father may be glorified in the Son." John
14:13.*

7. How else may Christians receive blessings from God?

A. *Christians may receive blessings from God by
helping others.*

"Blessed is he that considereth the poor: the Lord will
deliver him in time of trouble." Psalm 41:1.

*"I have shewed you all things, how that so laboring
ye ought to support the weak, and to remember the
words of the Lord Jesus, how he said, It is more
blessed to give than to receive." Acts 20:35.*

8. How else may Christians be blessed?

A. *Christians may receive blessings by paying
tithes.*

*"Bring ye all the tithes into the storehouse, that there
may be meat in mine house, and prove me now herewith, saith the Lord of hosts, if I will not open you
the windows of heaven, and pour you out a blessing,
that there shall not be room enough to receive it."
Malachi 3:10.*

III. A Christian's Relationship to Others

1. How does the Bible tell us to regard our parents?

A. *We should love, honor, and obey them.*

"Children, obey your parents in the Lord: for this is right. Honor thy father and mother." Ephesians 6:1, 2a.

"Honor thy father and thy mother: that thy days may be long upon the land which the Lord thy God giveth thee." Exodus 20:12.

2. How does the Bible tell us to regard such rulers as policemen, judges, governors?

A. *We should obey them.*

"Let every soul be subject unto the higher powers. For there is no power but of God; the powers that be are ordained of God. . . . For rulers are not a terror to good works, but to the evil." Romans 13:1, 3.

3. How does the Bible tell us to regard such leaders as our pastor and Sunday school teachers?

A. *We should be submissive unto them.*

"Obey them that have the rule over you, and submit yourselves: for they watch for your souls, as they that must give account, that they may do it with joy, and not with grief: for that is unprofitable for you." Hebrews 13:17.

4. How does the Bible tell us to regard other Christians?

A. *We should love them as Christ loves us.*

"A new commandment I give unto you, that ye love one another; as I have loved you, that ye also love one another. By this shall all men know that ye are my disciples, if ye have love one to another." John 13:34, 35.

5. How does the Bible tell us to regard our friends and neighbors?

A. *We should treat them as we would like to be treated.*

"As ye would that men should do to you, do ye also to them likewise." Luke 6:31.

"Love thy neighbor as thyself." Romans 13:9.

6. How does the Bible tell us to regard those that wrong us?

A. *We must love them and forgive them.*

"Love your enemies, bless them that curse you. Do good to them that hate you, and pray for them which despitefully use you and persecute you." *Matthew* 5:44.

"If ye forgive men their trespasses, your heavenly Father will also forgive you; but if ye forgive not men their trespasses, neither will your Father forgive your trespasses." Matthew 6:14, 15.

7. Does the Bible tell us how to regard the unsaved?

A. *Yes. We should show them by the way we act that Christ lives in us.*

"Let no man despise thy youth; but be thou an example of the believer, in word, in conversation, in charity, in spirit, in faith, in purity." *1 Timothy* 4:12.

"Let your light so shine before men, that they may see your good works, and glorify your Father which is in heaven. Matthew 5:16.

IV. A Christian and Himself

1. Does a Christian own his own life?

A. *No. The Lord owns the life of a Christian because He bought it with His own blood.*

"You were not redeemed with corruptible things, as silver and gold . . . but with the precious blood of Christ, as of a lamb without blemish and without spot." 1 Peter 1:18, 19.

2. What then should be a Christian's attitude toward his own life?

A. *He should glorify God in his body and in his spirit which are God's.*

"For ye are bought with a price: therefore glorify God in your body, and in your spirit, which are God's." 1 Corinthians 6:20.

3. What does the Bible say it will cost to be a Christian?

A. *The Bible tells us that to be a Christian means denying ourselves and taking up our cross and following Jesus.*

"*(Jesus said) If any man will come after me, let him deny himself, and take up his cross daily, and follow me.*" *Luke* 9:23.

4. What does it mean to deny ourselves?

A. *We deny ourselves when we do God's will rather than have our own way.*

"(Jesus said) I came down from heaven, not to do mine own will, but the will of him that sent me." John 6:38.

"Not every one that saith unto me, Lord, Lord, shall enter into the kingdom of heaven; but he that doeth the will of my Father which is in heaven." Matthew 7:21.

5. How does a Christian take up his cross daily?

A. *A Christian must choose to do right every day, even though it is contrary to what he naturally wants to do.*

"But put ye on the Lord Jesus Christ, and make not provision for the flesh, to fulfill the lusts thereof." Romans 13:14.

"I am crucified with Christ: nevertheless I live; yet not I, but Christ liveth in me, and the life which I now live in the flesh I live by the faith of the Son of God, who loved me, and gave himself for me." Galatians 2:20.

6. Why should a Christian keep his body and mind pure and clean?

A. *A Christian should keep his body and mind pure and clean because he is the temple of the Holy Ghost.*

"Know ye not that your body is the temple of the Holy Ghost which is in you, which ye have of God, and ye are not your own? You are bought with a price; therefore glorify God in your body, and in your spirit, which are God's." 1 Corinthians 6:19, 20.

7. Why are such habits as smoking and drinking defiling to the body?

A. *Smoking and drinking and other such habits are defiling because they are injurious to one's health, and they bring the body under their control.*

"If any man defile the temple of God, him shall God destroy." 1 Corinthians 3:17.

"Know ye not that to whom ye yield yourselves servants to obey, his servants ye are to whom ye obey; whether of sin unto death, or of obedience unto righteousness." Romans 6:16.

V. The Christian Life

1. What is the source of the Christian life?

A. *Christ Himself is the source of the Christian life.*

"To whom God would make known what is the riches of the glory of this mystery among the Gentiles; which is Christ in you, the hope of glory: Whereunto I also labor, striving according to his working, which worketh in me mightily." Colossians 1:27, 29.

2. Can we become Christians by doing good?

A. *No. We must be born into the family of God.*
"Marvel not that I said unto thee, Ye must be born again." John 3:7.

3. How can we be born into the family of God?

A. We can be born into the family of God by confessing our sins and accepting the Lord Jesus as our Saviour.

"He that believeth and is baptized shall be saved; but he that believeth not shall be damned." Mark 16:16.

4. How do we accept the Lord Jesus as our Saviour?

A. We accept the Lord Jesus as our Saviour by believing that God raised Him from the dead and by confessing Him before men.

"If thou shalt confess with thy mouth the Lord Jesus, and shalt believe in thine heart that God hath raised *him from the dead, thou shalt be saved. For with the heart man believeth unto righteousness; and with the mouth confession is made unto salvation."* Romans 10:9, 10.

5. How do we confess Christ before men?

A. *We confess Christ before men by testifying that He is our Saviour and by being baptized as He commanded.*

"*Whosoever therefore shall confess me before men, him will I confess also before my Father which is in heaven." Matthew* 10:32.

"*Go ye therefore, and teach all nations, baptizing them in the name of the Father, and of the Son, and of the Holy Ghost:* Teaching them to observe all things whatsoever I have commanded you: and, lo, I am with you alway, even unto the end of the world." Matthew 28:19, 20.

6. What else should we do to confess Christ?

A. *We should join the family of God which is the church.*

"*Praising God, and having favour with all the people. And the Lord added to the church daily such as should be saved."* "And of the rest durst no man join himself to them: but the people magnified them." Acts 2:47; 5:13.

7. What is the Christian's food?

A. *The word of God is the food by which Christians grow.*

"*As newborn babes, desire the sincere milk of the word that ye may grow thereby." 1 Peter* 2:2.

8. How often should a Christian pray?

A. (1) *A Christian should pray every day.*

"My voice shalt thou hear in the morning, O Lord; in the morning will I direct my prayer unto thee, and will look up." Psalm 5:3.

"*Evening, and morning, and at noon, will I pray, and cry aloud; and he shall hear my voice." Psalm* 55:17.

(2) *A Christian should be in an attitude of prayer at all times.*

"Pray without ceasing." 1 Thessalonians 5:17.

9. How often should a Christian read his Bible?

A. *A Christian should read his Bible every day.*

"Blessed is the man that walketh not in the counsel of the ungodly. . . . But his delight is in the law of the Lord; and in his law doth he meditate day and night." Psalm 1:1,2.

"O how love I thy law! It is my meditation all the day." Psalm 119:97.

10. Should a Christian memorize Scripture?

A. *Yes. For it is God's word which sanctifies the heart of the believer.*

"Thy word have I hid in mine heart, that I might not sin against thee." Psalm 119:11.

"Thy word is a lamp unto my feet, and a light unto my path." Psalm 119:105.

11. Should a Christian tell others about Christ?

A. *Yes. He should tell others about Christ for a Christian is the witness which God uses in the earth today.*

"Go ye into all the world ,and preach the gospel to every creature." Mark 16:15.

12. Does God have a claim on our thoughts?

A. *Yes. God's Word tells us that our thoughts make us what we are.*

"As he (a man) thinketh in his heart, so is he." Proverbs 23:7.

"And the peace of God which passeth all understanding, shall keep your *hearts* and *minds* through Christ Jesus." Philippians 4:7.

13. How can our thoughts be pleasing to God?

A. Our thoughts please God only when they are clean and pure.

"Finally, brethren, whatsoever things are true, whatsoever things are honest, whatsoever things are just, whatsoever things are pure, whatsoever things are lovely,

whatsoever things are of good report; if there be any virtue, and if there be any praise, think on these things." Philippians 4:8.

14. Should a Christian be careful about what he looks at?

A. *Yes. A Christian should be careful about the things he sees for the eyes are the windows of the soul.*

"The light of the body is the eye; if therefore thine eye be single, thy whole body shall be full of light." Matthew 6:22.

15. Should a Christian be careful about what he hears?

A. *Yes. A Christian should be careful about what he listens to because what he hears also enters his heart.*

"Take heed what ye hear." Mark 4:24.

16. Should a Christian be careful about what he reads?

A. *Yes. A Christian should be careful about what he reads, for what he reads also enters his heart.*

"This book of the law shall not depart out of thy mouth; but thou shalt meditate therein day and night, that thou mayest observe to do according to all that is written therein; for then thou shalt make thy way prosperous, and then thou shalt have good success." Joshua 1:8.

17. Should a Christian be careful about what he says?

A. *Yes. A Christian should be careful about what he says because a Christian influences others by what he says.*

"A soft answer turneth away wrath; but grievous words stir up anger. The tongue of the wise useth knowledge aright: but the mouth of fools poureth out foolishness. The eyes of the Lord are in every place, beholding the evil and the good. A wholesome tongue is a tree of life: but perverseness therein is a breach in the spirit." Proverbs 15:1-4.

"A word fitly spoken is like apples of gold in pictures of silver." Proverbs 25:11.

18. Should a Christian be careful about what he does?

A. *Yes. A Christian should be careful about what he does because God requires him to do right.*

"He hath shewed thee, O man, what is good; and what doth the Lord require of thee, but to do justly, and to love mercy, and to walk humbly with thy God." Micah 6:8.

19. Should a Christian be careful about his companions?

A. *Yes.   He should seek Christian companions and not attend places of worldly amusements.*

"Know ye not that the friendship of the world is enmity with God?   Whosoever therefore will be a friend of the world is the enemy of God." James 4:4.

20. Should a Christian attend church regularly?

A. *Yes.   A Christian should attend church regularly, because God's Word commands him to assemble with other Christians, especially during the last days.*

"Faith cometh by hearing and hearing by the word of God." Romans 10:17.

"Not forsaking the assembling of yourselves together, as the manner of some is; but exhorting one another: and so much the more, as ye see the day approaching. Hebrews 10:25.

21. Should a Christian support the church financially?

A. *Yes. A Christian should support the church because it is God's storehouse.*

"Bring ye all the tithes into the storehouse, that there may be meat in mine house, and prove me now herewith, saith the Lord of hosts, if I will not open you the windows of heaven, and pour you out a blessing, that there shall not be room enough to receive it." Malachi 3:10.

22. What is meant by tithing?

A. *Tithing is giving one tenth of one's income to the work of God.*

" . . . Abraham gave a tenth part of all." Hebrews 7:2.

23. Should a Christian pay tithes?

A. *Yes. The tithe has been God's portion from the beginning. The Pharisees tithed and Jesus said our righteousness should exceed their righteousness.*

"And this stone, which I have set for a pillar, shall be God's house: and of all that thou shalt give me I will surely give the tenth unto thee." Genesis 28:22.

"*For I say unto you, That except your righteousness shall exceed the righteousness of the scribes and Pharisees, ye shall in no case enter into the kingdom of heaven.*" *Matthew* 5:20.

"Woe unto you, scribes and Pharisees, hypocrites! For ye pay tithe of mint and anise and cummin, and have omitted the weightier matters of the law, judgment, mercy, and faith: these ought ye to have done, and not to leave the other undone." Matthew 23:23.

VI. The Spirit-filled Life

1. What is a Spirit-filled Life?

A. *A Spirit-filled life is one that is yielded and consecrated to God and thus filled with the Holy Spirit.*

"And be not drunk with wine, wherein is excess; but *be filled with the Spirit; speaking to yourselves in psalms and hymns and spiritual songs, singing and making melody in your heart to the Lord; giving thanks always for all things unto God and the Father in the name of our Lord Jesus Christ; submitting yourselves one to another in the fear of God.*" *Ephesians* 5:18-21.

2. How can a person live a Spirit-filled life?

A. *One may live a Spirit-filled life by becoming a born-again Christian first of all, and then by being baptized into the Holy Spirit and remaining under His anointing.*

"*Even the Spirit of truth; whom the world cannot receive, because it seeth him not, neither knoweth him:*

but ye know him; for he dwelleth with you, and shall be in you." John 14:17.

"For John truly baptized with water; but ye shall be baptized with the Holy Ghost not many days hence." Acts 1:5.

"The anointing which ye have received of him abideth in you, and ye need not that any man teach you: but as the same anointing teacheth you of all things, and is truth, and is no lie, and even as it hath taught you, ye shall abide in him." 1 John 2:27.

3. How can a Christian be baptized into the Holy Ghost?

A. *A Christian may be baptized into the Holy Ghost by tarrying in faith as the first disciples did, continually praising and blessing God.*

"Behold, I send the promise of my Father upon you: but tarry ye in the city of Jerusalem, until ye be endued with power from on high." "And (they) were continually in the temple, praising and blessing God." Luke 24:49, 53.

4. How may we know we have been filled with the Spirit?

A. *His power will come upon us as on the disciples on the day of Pentecost, and we will speak in other tongues as the Spirit gives utterance.*

"They were all filled with the Holy Ghost, and began to speak with other tongues, as the Spirit gave them utterance." Acts 2:4.

5. How may we remain under His anointing?

A. We may remain under His anointing by maintaining an attitude of obedience, yieldedness, faith and praise.

"See then that ye walk circumspectly, not as fools, but as wise, redeeming the time, because the days are evil. Wherefore be ye not unwise, but understanding what the will of the Lord is. And be not drunk with wine, wherein is excess; but be filled with the Spirit; speaking to yourselves in psalms and hymns and spiritual songs, singing and making melody in your heart to the Lord; giving thanks always for all things unto God

*and the Father in the name of our Lord Jesus Christ;
submitting yourselves one to another in the fear of
God."* *Ephesians 5:15-21.*

6. How else may we keep the presence of the Holy Spirit in our lives?

A. *We may keep the presence of the Holy Spirit
in our lives by not grieving the Spirit or
quenching the Spirit.*

*"And grieve not the Holy Spirit of God, whereby ye
are sealed unto the day of redemption." Ephesians 4:30.
"Quench not the Spirit." 1 Thessalonians 5:19.*

7. What are the characteristics of the Spirit-filled life?

A. Love, joy, peace, longsuffering, gentleness,
goodness, faith, meekness, temperance.

*"But the fruit of the Spirit is love, joy, peace, long-
suffering, gentleness, goodness, faith, meekness, temperance: against such there is no law." Galatians 5:
22, 23.*

8. Give another evidence of the Spirit's presence in such a life.

A. *The Spirit assists such a Christian in his
prayer life.*

*"Likewise the Spirit also helpeth our infirmities: for we
know not what we should pray for as we ought: but
the Spirit itself maketh intercession for us with groan-
ings which cannot be uttered." Romans 8:26.*

9. How else does the Holy Spirit minister to a Spirit-filled Christian?

A. *The Holy Spirit serves as a guide in his personal matters.*

*"For as many as are led by the Spirit of God, they
are the sons of God." Romans 8:14.*

"Now when they had gone throughout Phrygia and
the region of Galatia, and were forbidden of the Holy
Ghost to preach the word in Asia, after they were
come to Mysia, they assayed to go into Bithynia: but
the Spirit suffered them not." Acts 16:6, 7.

10. What is the Holy Spirit's relation to truth?

A. *He is the very Spirit of truth and is the great Teacher and guide into all truth.*

"But the Comforter, which is the Holy Ghost, whom the Father will send in my name, he shall teach you all things, and bring all things to your remembrance, whatsoever I have said unto you." John 14:26.

"Howbeit when he, the Spirit of truth, is come, he will guide you into all truth: for he shall not speak of himself; but whatsoever he shall hear, that shall he speak: and he will shew you things to come." John 16:13.

11. What can be said to be the chief purpose of the Baptism of the Holy Ghost?

A. *It is God's ordained plan and power for Christian service.*

"And, behold, I send the promise of my Father upon you: but tarry ye in the city of Jerusalem, until ye be endued with power from on high." Luke 24:49.

"But ye shall receive power, after that the Holy Ghost is come upon you: and ye shall be witnesses unto me both in Jerusalem, and in all Judea, and in Samaria, and unto the uttermost part of the earth." Acts 1:8.

12. What inward work does the Holy Spirit perform in the Spirit-filled life?

A. *He is the means of growth in our Christian life. He acts upon the soul to produce the virtues of Christian character.*

13. Does he make any special enduements for service available to us?

A. *Yes. He makes available the gifts of the Spirit.*

14. What are these gifts?

A. *The gifts of the Spirit are: the word of wisdom, the word of knowledge, faith, healing, miracles, prophecy, discerning of spirits, tongues, and interpretation of tongues.* 1 Corinthians 12:8-10.

15. What other gifts does the Spirit give to a Spirit-filled life?

A. *The Holy Spirit gives the ability to teach, to exhort, to be generous, to rule, and to show mercy.*

"Having then gifts differing according to the grace that is given to us, . . . *let us prophesy according to the proportion of faith; or ministry, let us wait on our ministering, or he that teacheth, on teaching; or he that exhorteth, on exhortation; he that giveth, let him do it with simplicity; he that ruleth, with diligence; he that sheweth mercy, with cheerfulness.*" Romans **12:6-8.**

PART 3
Bible Doctrine for Adults

ADULT DOCTRINE

I. The Bible

1. How popular is the Bible?

A. The Bible is the world's best-selling book.

2. Why is the Bible so popular?

A. It meets the need of the human heart and is the only true answer to the questions of the soul and of eternity.

3. How old is the Bible?

A. The first book of the Bible was written about 1500 B.C. and the last book of the New Testament about A.D. 100. It is thus the oldest book in existence today.

4. How many authors of the Bible are there?

A. There are about 40 human authors of the Bible who wrote at different times and places without conferring together.

5. Who is the real Author of the Bible?

A. The Holy Spirit of God is the divine Author of the Bible, for these holy men of God spoke as they were moved of the Holy Ghost.

"For the prophecy came not in old time by the will of man; but holy men of God spake as they were moved by the Holy Ghost." 2 Peter 1:21.

6. Did the Holy Spirit write any books other than the ones contained in the Bible?

A. No. The Bible is the only book in the world today that is wholly inspired of God.

"All scripture is given by inspiration of God, and is profitable for doctrine, for reproof, for correction, for instruction in righteousness." 2 Timothy 3:16.

7. How do we know that the Bible is inspired like no other book?

A. We know that the Bible is inspired because of its perfect unity in spite of its great diversity. Its unity is organic, structural, historical, and doctrinal; and its diversity appears in many human authors, in the languages in which it was written, in the different literary forms and styles used in its writings, and in the circumstances and time of the writing of each of its various books.

8. Are there other reasons for believing the Bible is divinely inspired?

A. Yes. The high moral character of its writers and its teachings, its many remarkable prophecies which have been fulfilled, its agelong indestructibility, and its demonstrated agreement with approved science.

9. Is every word of the Bible inspired?

A. Yes. Every word is inspired in the original manuscripts, but because of many copyings and translations a few slight inaccuracies have resulted in these translations.

"Which things also we speak, not in the words which man's wisdom teacheth, but which the Holy Ghost teacheth; comparing spiritual things with spiritual." 1 Corinthians 2:13.

"For this cause also thank we God without ceasing, because, when ye received the word of God which ye heard of us, ye received it not as the word of men, but as it is in truth, the word of God, which effectually worketh also in you that believe." 1 Thessalonians 2:13.

10. Are these inaccuracies serious?

A. No. For no vital doctrine has been affected by these variations. Most of them are being eliminated by recent discoveries of older manuscripts.

II. God

1. How do we know there is a God?

A. We know there is a God because all effects must have a cause. In creation all about us we see tremendous effects or phenomena. These effects must have a great Cause. We call this Cause God. A creator must be superior to the things which he creates. Cf. Psalm 19; 139:1-16.

2. Are there other reasons for believing there is a God?

A. Yes. Someone must have deliberately designed all the laws and marvels of nature and life. There is no possibility that all these things could have come into existence by chance. Design implies a designer and must have a Designer. Cf. Job 38 and 39; Proverbs 8:22-30.

3. Is it instinctive in man to believe in God?

A. Yes. All nations believe in some superior being or god and only a fool says, "There is no God." Cf. Psalm 14:1.

4. What are the natural attributes of God?

A. The natural attributes of God are eternality, omnipotence, omniscience, omnipresence, and glory. Cf. Deuteronomy 33:27; Psalm 90:2; Daniel 4:35; Isaiah 46:9, 10; Psalm 139:7-12; John 17:5.

5. Name some of His moral attributes.

A. Some of the moral attributes of God are love, faithfulness, impartiality, mercy, goodness, justice, holiness, truthfulness, long suffering, and humility. Cf. John 4:8; 1 Corinthians 1:9; 1 Peter 1:17; Psalm 103:17; Psalm

107:8; Revelation 15:3; 1 Peter 1:15, 16;
Isaiah 25:1; Psalm 86:15; Isaiah 66:1, 2.

6. Can anyone excel God in any of these virtues?

A. No. The conception of God is the conception
of a Being, a greater than whom cannot be
conceived. Cf. Exodus 3:14; Jeremiah 32:17,
18, 27.

7. Is there one God or many?

A. There is only one God and He has existed
from all eternity in three persons: Father,
Son and Holy Spirit. These Three are one
God, the same in substance, equal in power
and glory.

"Hear, O Israel: The Lord our God is one Lord."
Deuteronomy 6:4.

"Unto thee it was shewed, that thou mightest know
that the Lord he is God; there is none else beside him."
Deuteronomy 4:35.

"But to us there is but one God, the Father, of whom
are all things, and we in him; and one Lord Jesus
Christ, by whom are all things, and we by him."
1 Corinthians 8:6. Cf. John 8:58; Hebrews 13:8;
Revelation 1:4; 4:8.

"There is one body, and one Spirit, even as ye are
called in one hope of your calling; One Lord, one faith,
one baptism, one God and Father of all, who is above
all, and through all, and in you all." Ephesians 4:4-6.

8. What is the relationship between these three Persons?

A. The Father begat the Son, the Son is begotten
of the Father; and the Holy Ghost proceeds
from the Father and the Son. These three
are equal with each other, for all have ascribed
to them such names, attributes, works, and
worship as are proper to God only. Cf. John
1:14, 16, 18; 8:42; 13:3; 15:26; 16:13-16,
27, 28; Hebrews 9:14.

III. Man

1. How was the world created?

A. The world was created by the spoken Word of God. The worlds were framed by the Word of God so that things which are seen were not made of things which do appear.

"Through faith we understand that the worlds were framed by the word of God, so that things which are seen were not made of things which do appear." Hebrews 11:3.

2. Did God cause a substance or thing to evolve into a plant or an animal?

A. There is no evidence in the fossils or rocks or in nature or life of any kind today that any species ever developed into another species.

3. Is there any scripture that refutes the theory of evolution?

A. Yes. Genesis 1:11 and 24 say that God made every herb after its kind with its seed in itself and every living creature after his kind.

4. How was man created?

A. Man was created in the likeness and image of God.

"And God said, Let us make man in our image, after our likeness: and let them have dominion over the fish of the sea, and over the fowl of the air, and over the cattle, and over all the earth, and over every creeping thing that creepeth upon the earth. So God created man in his own image, in the image of God created he him; male and female created he them." Genesis 1:26-27. Cf. also Ephesians 4:24.

5. What is meant by the likeness and image of God?

A. Man is tripartite (spirit, soul and body) like God is triune (Father, Son and Holy Spirit); his will is inviolate, like God's; and he, too, will endure forever. In his original creation, man was perfectly holy and blest.

6. What was man's relation to God in the Garden of Eden?

A. Man was loyal and obedient to God and had communion with Him.

"And the Lord God took the man, and put him into the garden of Eden to dress it and to keep it. And they heard the voice of the Lord God walking in the garden in the cool of the day." Genesis 2:15; 3:8a.

7. What was man's relation to the rest of God's creation?

A. He was given dominion over all animals and over all of God's creation.

"And God said, Let us make man in our image, after our likeness: and let them have dominion over the fish of the sea, and over the fowl of the air, and over the cattle, and over all the earth, and over every creeping thing that creepeth upon the earth." Genesis 1:26.

8. Were there any restrictions placed upon man in the Garden of Eden?

A. He was commanded not to eat of the tree of the knowledge of good and evil.

"But of the tree of the knowledge of good and evil, thou shalt not eat of it: for in the day that thou eatest thereof thou shalt surely die." Genesis 2:17.

9. Why was he given this restriction?

A. He was given this restriction to test his loyalty to God and to permit the operation of his free will.

10. Did man remain true to God and choose to obey Him?

A. There was unbroken communion between God and man until man's fall.

"And they heard the voice of the Lord God walking in the garden in the cool of the day; and Adam and his wife hid themselves from the presence of the Lord God amongst the trees of the garden." Genesis 3:8.

IV. Sin

1. How did sin begin in God's universe?

A. Lucifer, one of the heavenly cherubim, became proud and rebelled against God.

"How art thou fallen from heaven, O Lucifer, son of the morning! how art thou cut down to the ground, which didst weaken the nations! For thou hast said in thine heart, I will ascend into heaven, I will exalt my throne above the stars of God: I will sit also upon the mount of the congregation, in the sides of the north: I will ascend above the heights of the clouds; I will be like the most High." Isaiah 14:12-14. Cf. also Ezekiel 28:12-15.

2. What was the result of that rebellion?

A. Lucifer was deposed and with his followers was cast out of heaven.

"Yet thou shalt be brought down to hell, to the sides of the pit." Isaiah 14:15. Cf. also Jude 6.

3. What became of Lucifer?

A. He became known as Satan and is now the god of this world.

"In whom the god of this world hath blinded the minds of them which believe not, lest the light of the glorious gospel of Christ, who is the image of God, should shine unto them." 2 Corinthians 4:4. Cf. also Revelation 20:2.

4. Did he interfere with God's creation in Eden?

A. Yes. He appeared to Eve in the form of a serpent and tempted her to disobey God by eating of the forbidden tree.

"But I fear, lest by any means, as the serpent beguiled Eve through his subtilty, so your minds should be corrupted from the simplicity that is in Christ." 2 Corinthians 11:3.

5. What methods did Satan use in tempting Eve?

A. He created doubt in her heart toward God concerning His kindness in denying them the tree of the knowledge of good an evil, and he awakened pride in her heart in an ambition to be like God.

"Now the serpent was more subtil than any beast of the field which the Lord God had made. And he said unto the woman, Yea, hath God said, Ye shall not eat of every tree of the garden? For God doth know that in the day ye eat thereof, then your eyes shall be opened, and ye shall be as gods, knowing good and evil." Genesis 3:1, 5.

6. Were Satan's methods effective?

A. Yes. He succeeded in causing her to sin; and unbelief and pride have been the root-cause of sin ever since.

"And when the woman saw that the tree was good for food, and that it was pleasant to the eyes, and a tree to be desired to make one wise, she took of the fruit thereof, and did eat, and gave also unto her husband with her; and he did eat." Genesis 3:6.

7. What was Eve's first act after sinning?

A. She persuaded her husband also to sin. It is characteristic of sinners to lead others into sin. Cf. Gen. 3:6.

8. Why did Adam sin?

A. Adam was not deceived, as Eve was, but preferred his wife to obedience to God.

"And Adam was not deceived, but the woman being deceived was in the transgression." 1 Timothy 2:14.

9. What basic law did he thus break?

A. The first and great commandment: "Thou shalt love the Lord thy God with all thy heart, and with all thy soul, and with all thy mind." Matthew 22:37.

10. What was God's attitude toward His creatures who had sinned?

A. He came looking for them. He always is seeking to save those who are lost.

"And the Lord God called unto Adam, and said unto him, Where art thou?" Genesis 3:9.

"For the Son of man is come to seek and to save that which was lost." Luke 19:10.

11. What was the attitude of our first parents toward God after their sin?

A. They hid from Him. All sinners try to hide from God.

"And they heard the voice of the Lord God walking in the garden in the cool of the day: and Adam and his wife hid themselves from the presence of the Lord God amongst the trees of the garden." Genesis 3:8.

12. What steps in their fall are clearly seen?

A. They saw, they coveted, they took, and they hid. These are the usual steps downward into sin.

"And when the woman saw that the tree was good for food, and that it was pleasant to the eyes, and a tree to be desired to make one wise, she took of the fruit thereof, and did eat, and gave also unto her husband with her; and he did eat." Genesis 3:6.

"When I *saw* among the spoils a goodly Babylonish garment, and two hundred shekels of silver, and a wedge of gold of fifty shekels weight, then I *coveted* them, and *took* them; and, behold, they are hid in the earth in the midst of my tent, and the silver under it." Joshua 7:21.

13. What were the results of their sin?

A. Their understanding became darkened, their hearts became wicked, and their bodies became subject to disease and death.

"Having the understanding darkened, being alienated from the life of God through the ignorance that is in them, because of the blindness of their heart." Ephesians 4:18. Cf. also Jeremiah 17:9; Genesis 2:17; 3:19.

14. Were there other results of their fall?

A. Yes. All nature was cursed for their sake, they were deposed from rulership over nature, and expelled from the Garden of Eden and from the presence of God.

"And unto Adam he said, Because thou hast hearkened unto the voice of thy wife, and hast eaten of the tree, of which I commanded thee, saying, Thou shalt not eat of it: cursed is the ground for thy sake; in sorrow shalt thou eat of it all the days of thy life; thorns also and thistles shall it bring forth to thee; and thou shalt eat the herb of the field; in the sweat of thy face shalt thou eat bread, till thou return unto the ground; for out of it wast thou taken: for dust thou art, and unto dust shalt thou return." Genesis 3:17-19.

15. Did their fall affect the human race?

A. Yes. Through Adam sin entered into the world and death by sin; and since all have sinned, all suffer the results of sin.

"Wherefore, as by one man sin entered into the world, and death by sin; and so death passed upon all men, for that all have sinned." Romans 5:12.

16. What is the eternal destiny of sinners?

A. They shall be punished with everlasting destruction from the presence of the Lord and shall have their part in the lake which burneth with fire and brimstone.

"Behold, all souls are mine; as the soul of the father, so also the soul of the son is mine: the soul that sinneth, it shall die." Ezekiel 18:4.

"But the fearful, and unbelieving, and the abominable, and murderers, and whoremongers, and sorcerers, and idolaters, and all liars, shall have their part in the lake which burneth with fire and brimstone: which is the second death." Revelation 21:8. Cf. also 2 Thessalonians 1:9; Revelation 20:10, 15.

17. Is there any deliverance from sin and its consequences?

A. Yes. Through the confession of sin, the acceptance of the forgiveness of sins through the atoning death of Jesus Christ, and the confession of Christ as personal Saviour.

"That if thou shalt confess with thy mouth the Lord Jesus, and shalt believe in thine heart that God hath raised him from the dead, thou shalt be saved. For with the heart man believeth unto righteousness; and with the mouth confession is made unto salvation." Romans 10:9, 10.

V. JESUS CHRIST

1. When did Christ begin to exist?

A. Christ has always existed, co-eternally with God the Father.

"In the beginning was the Word, and the Word was with God, and the Word was God. The same was in the beginning with God." John 1:1, 2.

2. Do the Scriptures tell of the relation between the Father and the Son from the beginning?

A. Yes. The Scriptures declare that the Son was with the Father in the beginning, that they shared the divine glory before the world was, and that the Father loved the Son before the foundation of the world.

"And now, O Father, glorify thou me with thine own self with the glory which I had with thee before the world was. Father, I will that they also, whom thou hast given me, be with me where I am; that they may behold my glory, which thou hast given me: for thou lovedst me before the foundation of the world." John 17:5, 24. Cf. also John 1:1, 2.

3. By whom was heaven itself created?

A. Christ made heaven and its throne, and all the angels.

"Who is the image of the invisible God, the firstborn of every creature: For by him were all things created, that are in heaven, and that are in earth, visible and invisible, whether they be thrones, or dominions, or principalities or powers: all things were created by him, and for him." Colossians 1:15, 16.

"All things were made by him: and without him was not any thing made that was made." John 1:3.

4. By whom was the world created?

A. Christ was the Agent of creation, although God the Father and the Holy Spirit were active in creation also.

"All things were made by him; and without him was not any thing made that was made." John 1:3.

"In the beginning God created the heaven and the earth. And the earth was without form, and void; and darkness was upon the face of the deep. And the Spirit of God moved upon the face of the waters." Genesis 1:1, 2. Cf. also Hebrews 1:2.

5. Why did God create the world?

A. God made the world to the praise of the glory of His Son. All things were made by Him and for Him and to Him, to whom be glory forever. Amen.

"For of him, and through him, and to him, are all things: to whom be glory for ever. Amen." Romans 11:36.

6. Did Christ reveal Himself to man in the Old Testament times?

A. Some think that it was Christ as "the angel of the Lord," who appeared to Abraham, Jacob, Moses, Joshua, Gideon and Manoah. Cf. Genesis 17:1; 18:1, 2; Genesis 32:24-30; Exodus 14:19; Joshua 5:13-15; Judges 6; Judges 13:2-7.

7. Were the offices and ministries of Christ typified in the Old Testament?

A. Yes. Priests, kings, and prophets were typical of the threefold office and ministry of Christ. Cf. Hebrews 9; Deut. 18:5; Jeremiah 23:5.

8. What is meant by the incarnation of Christ?

A. When Christ laid aside His glory, came down from heaven, and was born of the Virgin Mary, He became flesh, or God incarnate (embodied or clothed) in human flesh.

"And the Word was made flesh, and dwelt among us, (and we behold his glory, the glory as of the only begotten of the Father,) full of grace and truth." John 1:14.

9. Did Christ lose His essential deity when He became flesh?

A. No. He merely laid aside His outward glory and became subject to the limitations of the flesh, or a human life.

"Who, being in the form of God, thought it not robbery to be equal with God: But made himself of no reputation, and took upon him the form of a servant, and was made in the likeness of man." Philippians 2:6-7.

10. Did He gain anything by His incarnation?

A. He took upon Him the form and the nature of man, in order to redeem man.

"And being found in fashion as a man, he humbled himself, and became obedient unto death, even the death of the cross." Philippians 2:8.

11. Did Jesus inherit a sinful human nature from His mother?

A. No. A special body was prepared Him in which was no sin.

"Wherefore when he cometh into the world, he saith, Sacrifice and offering thou wouldest not, but a body hast thou prepared me." Hebrews 10:5.

12. Was His mother also without sin?

A. No. She acknowledged her need of a Saviour.

"And Mary said, My Soul doth magnify the Lord, and my spirit hath rejoiced in God my Saviour." Luke 1:46, 47.

13. Did Jesus then have two natures?

A. Yes. He was true God and true man, united in the One Person of Christ in one personal consciousness.

"Concerning his Son Jesus Christ our Lord, which was made of the seed of David according to the flesh;

And declared to be the Son of God with power, according to the spirit of holiness, by the resurrection from the dead." Romans 1:3, 4.

14. Did Jesus know all things immediately and instinctively or did He have to learn?

A. Jesus learned obedience and increased in wisdom as He did in stature.

"And the child grew, and waxed strong in spirit, filled with wisdom: and the grace of God was upon him. And Jesus increased in wisdom and stature, and in favour with God and man." Luke 2:40, 52.

15. Was it necessary for Jesus to be baptized in water?

A. Only to fulfill all righteousness and to serve as our Leader and Example.

"And Jesus answering said unto him, Suffer it to be so now; for thus it becometh us to fulfill all righteousness. Then he suffered him." Matthew 3:15.

16. What was the significance of the Holy Spirit's descending from heaven, lighting upon Him, and remaining on Him?

A. This was Christ's anointing and equipment for the mighty ministry which He performed.

"How God anointed Jesus of Nazareth with the Holy Ghost and with power: who went about doing good, and healing all that were oppressed of the devil; for God was with him." Acts 10:38. Cf. also Isaiah 61:1-3.

17. Of what did His ministry chiefly consist?

A. His ministry consisted of His marvelous teachings, His miraculous deeds, and the divine character and nature which He displayed.

18. How can Christ's unique ministry be accounted for?

A. Only by the fact that he was (and is) the Son of God.

19. How early was Jesus conscious that God was His Father?

A. At the age of twelve He said "Wist ye not that I must be about my Father's business?" Luke 2:49.

20. When did Jesus reveal that He was the Son of God?

A. At the very beginning of His ministry, He accepted John's designation as the Messiah.

"The next day John seeth Jesus coming unto him, and saith, Behold the Lamb of God, which taketh away the sin of the world." "And I knew him not: but he that sent me to baptize with water, the same said unto me, Upon whom thou shalt see the Spirit descending, and remaining on him, the same is he which baptizeth with the Holy Ghost." John 1:29, 33.

21. On what occasions did He say He was the Son of God?

A. To the woman of Samaria, to the man born blind, to His disciples, to the Pharisees, and to the high priest. Cf. John 4:25, 26; 9:35-38; Matthew 16:15-17; John 8:54-58; Mark 14:61, 62.

22. What evidence was there that Jesus was the Son of God?

A. He demonstrated the attributes of Deity: Omnipotence, omniscience, and omnipresence, as well as God's love, humility, and holiness. Cf. Matthew 14:19-21; John 11:14; Matthew 18:20; Luke 23:34; John 13:3, 4; John 8:46.

23. What was the chief purpose of Christ's incarnation?

A. Christ's chief purpose in coming into this world was to redeem the world by His death on the cross.

"Even as the Son of man came not to be ministered unto, but to minister, and to give his life a ransom for many." Matthew 20:28.

24. How could His death redeem the world?

A. Humanity was condemned to die because of its sin. Christ, the sinless One, chose to die in its place.

"For Christ also hath once suffered for sins, the just for the unjust, that he might bring us to God, being

put to death in the flesh, but quickened by the Spirit."
1 Peter 3:18.

25. Has the world now been delivered from death?

A. The price of deliverance has been paid, but
each individual must accept that deliverance
for himself.

"For therefore we both labour and suffer reproach,
because we trust in the living God, who is the Saviour
of all men, specially of those that believe." 1 Timothy
4:10.

**26. What part did the resurrection of Christ have in
our redemption?**

A. The resurrection of Christ was the seal of
God's acceptance of Christ's atoning work and
the proof of our completed redemption.

"And declared to be the Son of God with power,
according to the spirit of holiness, by the resurrection
from the dead." Romans 1:4.

"And if Christ be not raised, your faith is vain: ye
are yet in your sins." 1 Corinthians 15:17.

**27. What proofs are there that Jesus was raised from
the dead?**

A. The empty tomb, the testimony of the angels,
His ten appearances to His disciples, the moral
transformation in the disciples, and His revelation to Stephen, Paul and John. Cf. John
20; 1 Corinthians 15:5-8; Acts 7:55, 56;
Acts 9:1-6; Revelation 1:12-17.

**28. What is the most convincing proof of Christ's resur-
rection to Christians today?**

A. His presence and power within their hearts
and lives.

"To whom God would make known what is the riches
of the glory of this mystery among the Gentiles: which
is Christ in you, the hope of glory." Colossians 1:27.

29. What is the significance of Christ's ascension?

A. He ascended into heaven and entered into the

holy place to present the evidences of the perfect sacrifice of His own blood. He was crowned with glory and honor and then sat down on the right hand of God.

"Neither by the blood of goats and calves, but by his own blood he entered in once into the holy place, having obtained eternal redemption for us." Hebrews 9:12.

"But this man, after he had offered one sacrifice for sins for ever, sat down on the right hand of God." Hebrews 10:12.

30. What is Christ doing now?

A. Christ as our High Priest, is interceding for His own, serving as the only Mediator between God and man.

"Wherefore he is able also to save them to the uttermost that come unto God by him, seeing he ever liveth to make intercession for them." Hebrews 7:25.

"For Christ is not entered into the holy places made with hands, which are the figures of the true; but into heaven itself, now to appear in the presence of God for us." Hebrews 9:24. Cf. also 1 Timothy 2:5.

VI. Salvation

1. Are some men predestined (destined ahead of time) to be saved and others to be lost?

A. No, not in the aboslute sense. Predestination would limit Christ's atonement, and He died for all. It would nullify man's free will and amount to fatalism, which is gross error. Salvation is always for "whosoever will."

"For God so loved the world, that he gave his only begotten Son, that whosoever believeth in him should not perish, but have everlasting life." John 3:16. Cf. 1 Timothy 4:10; Revelation 22:17.

2. Why then does the Bible speak of predestination?

A. "Whom He did foreknow, He also did predestinate" (Romans 8:29) ties predestination with foreknowledge and thus gives it its proper limitation. He had to know everything in advance (otherwise He would be limited and God cannot be limited in knowledge) and this naturally included the knowledge that some men would accept and that some would reject His salvation. But God, in His all-power and all-wisdom, has left man absolutely free to make his own choice. Otherwise He would not (could not, for He is inherently just) punish men for what it is inevitable that they should do. God's sovereignty and man's free will are both truths taught by the Bible and both exist and operate simultaneously and without contradiction.

3. If Christ died for all men, then are all men saved?

A. Christ died on behalf of all men, making possible the salvation of all men. He also desires the salvation of all men; but man is a free moral agent, and each man must decide for himself if he will accept the free gift of everlasting life.

"The next day John seeth Jesus coming unto him, and saith, Behold the Lamb of God, which taketh away the sin of the world." John 1:29.

"And he is the propitiation for our sins: and not for ours only, but also for the sins of the whole world." 1 John 2:2.

"Who will have all men to be saved, and to come unto the knowledge of the truth." 1 Timothy 2:4.

"The Lord is not slack concerning his promise, as some men count slackness; but is longsuffering to us-ward, not willing that any should perish, but that all should come to repentance." 2 Peter 3:9.

"And he said unto them, Go ye into all the world, and preach the gospel to every creature. He that believeth and is baptized shall be saved; but he that believeth not shall be damned." Mark 16:15, 16.

4. Who takes the initiative in a person's salvation?

A. The Holy Spirit convicts of sin, grants repentance, and imparts everlasting life. It is thus by grace we are saved—not of works, but through faith in God.

"And when he is come, he will reprove the world of sin, and of righteousness, and of judgment." John 16:8.

"When they heard these things, they held their peace, and glorified God, saying, Then hath God also to the Gentiles granted repentance unto life." Acts 11:18. Cf. also John 3:5.

"For by grace are ye saved through faith; and that not of yourselves: it is the gift of God: not of works, lest any man should boast." Ephesians 2:8, 9.

5. What is man's part in his salvation?

A. He must receive a love for the truth (2 Thessalonians 2:10), must believe the gospel (Mark 16:16) and must receive Christ into his heart (John 1:12, 13).

6. What now becomes his attitude toward sin?

A. He will repent of his sins (regret them), confess them (acknowledge them), forsake them (cease doing them) and where possible, make restitution for them (for example, restore that which has been stolen, etc.).

7. What happens in a man's heart at conversion?

A. He is raised from spiritual death (Ephesians 2:5), receives divine life into his soul (1 Peter 1:4), and becomes a new creature in Christ (2 Corinthians 5:17).

8. At conversion, is a man born into the family of God or adopted into that family?

A. Both. He actually becomes a partaker of God's

nature, inheriting his Father's qualities, and is also legally adopted into God's family and made an heir of God, and a joint-heir with Christ.

"And if children, then heirs; heirs of God, and joint-heirs with Christ; if so be that we suffer with him, that we may be also glorified together." Romans 8:17. Cf. also Galatians 1:5; Ephesians 4:5.

9. What is the significance of justification?

A. Justification is a part of salvation which takes place in heaven when a man is saved. It is the act of God, the great Judge, in acquitting the sinner because that sinner has accepted Christ's death as a substitute for his own in penalty for his sins.   God also imputes, or reckons to the forgiven sinner's credit the merit and righteousness of His own Son.   By God's decree all guilt is gone, and in its place the great moral wealth of Christ is bestowed as a free gift.

10. Are there legal grounds upon which God can do this?

A. Yes. He is both just and the justifier of him that believeth in Jesus because full satisfaction for sin and an immense moral credit has been filed in the court of heaven by the death of the Son of God.   It is the gracious will of God the Father and His Son that that credit be placed to the account of us undeserving sinners.

"To declare, I say, at this time his righteousness: that he might be just, and the justifier of him which believeth in Jesus." Romans 3:26.

"If we confess our sins, he is faithful and *just* to forgive us our sins, and to cleanse us from all unrighteousness." 1 John 1:9.

11. Is sanctification also a part of salvation?

A. Yes. Sanctification is God's plan for dealing with the sin principle in man's life.

"For this is the will of God, even your sanctification." 1 Thessalonians 4:3.

12. How does this plan operate?

A. On God's side, Christ took man's sinful nature (the "old man") to the cross with Him when He died there. He not only died to atone for man's deeds of sin which were past, but to provide an escape from the power of sin by destroying the very body of sin on the cross.

"Whom God hath set forth to be a propitiation through faith in his blood, to declare his righteousness for the remission of sins that are past, through the forebearance of God." Romans 3:25.

"Knowing this, that our old man is crucified with him, that the body of sin might be destroyed, that henceforth we should not serve sin." Romans 6:6.

13. Does man have a part in this plan other than to accept it?

A. No and yes. He merely accepts, but that acceptance involves a "fight of faith." He must see and accept that his old self—the sinning nature—is crucified with Christ, he must "reckon" it there and persist in holding it there by faith, and must refuse to yield his members (any part of his being) to sin. This results in a breaking of its power that "henceforth we should not serve sin." Cf. Romans 6:6-14.

14. Does this complete the work of sanctification in one's life?

A. No. There is also a positive side of sanctification. The new man must take the place of the old man. We put off the one and put on the other. While we reckon the old man dead, we reckon the new man alive; and in inverse proportion it takes place. We refuse to yield to sin, to obey it in the lusts thereof; but we choose to yield ourselves to God and our members as instruments of righteousness to God.

"Likewise reckon ye also yourselves to be dead indeed unto sin, but alive unto God through Jesus Christ our Lord. Neither yield ye your members as instruments of unrighteousness unto sin: but yield yourselves unto God, as those that are alive from the dead, and your members as instruments of righteousness unto God." Romans 6:11, 13. Cf. also Colossians 3:8-14.

15. Is there another scriptural way of describing this experience?

A. Yes. It is identification with Christ in His death and resurrection. We died with Him to dispose of sin and its power, and we rose with Him to walk in newness of life.

"Therefore we are buried with him by baptism into death: that like as Christ was raised up from the dead by the glory of the Father, even so we also should walk in newness of life." Romans 6:4.

16. What else was nailed with Jesus to the cross?

A. Man's sickness and disease. Deliverance from the power of sickness was bought and secured for us in the same way that deliverance from sin was purchased and effected.

"But he was wounded for our transgressions, he was bruised for our iniquities: the chastisement of our peace was upon him; and with his stripes we are healed." Isaiah 53:5. Cf. also Matthew 8:17; 1 Peter 2:24.

17. Does this mean we can be healed from our sicknesses as we can be saved from our sins?

A. It surely does. At the Fountain of Calvary we can be sanctified in spirit, soul and body.

"And the very God of peace sanctify you wholly; and I pray God your whole spirit and soul and body be preserved blameless unto the coming of our Lord Jesus Christ." 1 Thessalonians 5:23.

18. What else was accomplished at Calvary for us?

A. The handwriting of ordinances was nailed to the cross (Colossians 2:14); the world too was crucified there (Galatians 6:14); and the power of Satan also was for us destroyed by Jesus' death.

"For as much then as the children are partakers of flesh and blood, he also himself likewise took part of the same; that through death he might destroy him that had the power of death, that is, the devil." Hebrews 2:14.

19. Were all of these things included in our redemption?

A. Yes, and more. Our bodies will at last be resurrected or raptured and we will stand in glorified bodies before His throne. Cf. Romans 8:19-23.

20. How can these phases of salvation conveniently be summarized?

A. By placing them in two groups: things done in heaven and things done on earth. In the first group are justification, adoption and what God did at Calvary to provide sanctification and healing. On man's side (which must be done on earth) are repentance, regeneration, and the acceptance of sanctification and healing.

21. What part does faith have in redemption?

A. "Without faith it is impossible to please God." At the very beginning, he that cometh to God must believe that He is and that He is a rewarder of them that diligently seek Him. By faith are we saved and we are kept by the power of God through faith. It is the prayer of faith that saves the sick. We receive the promise of the Spirit through faith, and by faith we will be translated at last. "All things are possible to him that believeth." "According to your faith be it unto you." Cf. Hebrews 11:6; Ephesians 2:8; James 5:15; Matthew 9:29.

22. If we are saved by faith and not by works, then why does James say, "That by works a man is justified and not by faith only?" James 2:24.

A. James himself explains the apparent contradiction as follows: "Faith wrought with his (Abraham's) works, and by works was faith made perfect." James 2:22. "I will shew thee my faith by my works." v. 18. For our faith to be alive and real, we must "act" like, we believe and those actions (or works) will express and prove our faith. These are the works that please God rather than the work done as merit or claimed as righteousness.

23. What is the place and importance of prayer?

A. Prayer is the language of the soul in speaking to God. Through prayer a sinner makes his peace with God and the saint communes with his Saviour. It is also the medium whereby the Christian gets things from God, for himself and for the extension of God's kingdom. Cf. Psalms 5; 141:2.

24. Repeat what is known as the Lord's prayer.

"Our Father which art in heaven,
Hallowed be thy name.

Thy kingdom come.
Thy will be done in earth, as it is in heaven.
Give us this day our daily bread.
And forgive us our debts, as we forgive our debtors.
And lead us not into temptation, but deliver us from evil:
For thine is the kingdom, and the power, and the glory, forever. Amen."—Matthew 6:9-13.

25. What part does fasting play in a Christian's life?

A. Fasting should never be entered upon for merit or "works." It is rather practiced as an aid to concentration on prayer. Cf. Matthew 17:21; Isaiah 58:6, 7; Acts 13:2, 3.

26. Is there any danger of a person ever being lost after once having been truly born again?

A. A person does not lose his freedom of will after being saved. He has the gift of eternal life but may return the gift and become as he was before receiving it. By faith he became saved and by subsequent unbelief he may become lost. No man is able to pluck one of Christ's sheep out of the Father's hand, but he may definitely remove himself out of His hand. Unbelief and unconfessed sin persisted in will damn any soul. "They could not enter in because of unbelief." Hebrews 3:19. Cf. also Colossians 1:23; Hebrews 3:6, 14; James 5:19, 20; Revelation 3:5.

VII. The Holy Spirit

1. How do we know that the Holy Spirit is a Person?

A. Jesus referred to Him as the Person who would take His place with the disciples. He is called "another Comforter" like Jesus was. The qualities of a person are attributed to Him, such as intelligence, emotion, and will.

Personal activities are ascribed to Him such as teaching (John 14:26); witness (Galatians 4:6); and intercession (Romans 8:26), etc. Cf. also John 14:6, 26; 15:26; Ephesians 4:30; 1 Corinthians 12:11.

2. What is the ministry of the Holy Spirit in the world?

A. He has come to persuade all men to accept the redemption which Jesus died to provide for them. Cf. John 16:8-13.

3. Does the Holy Spirit minister to sinners or to believers?

A. The Holy Spirit ministers to both sinners and believers. He convicts sinners of their sins and guides believers into all truth.

"And when he is come, he will reprove the world of sin, and of righteousness, and of judgment: Howbeit when he, the Spirit of truth, is come, he will guide you into all truth: for he shall not speak of himself; but whatsoever he shall hear, that shall he speak: and he will shew you things to come." John 16:8, 13.

4. Into what two phases can the work of the Holy Spirit in believers' lives be divided?

A. Believers are born of the Spirit in the first place and they are baptized into the Spirit in the second place.

"Jesus answered, Verily, verily, I say unto thee, Except a man be born of the water and of the Spirit, he cannot enter into the Kingdom of God." John 3:5.

"For John truly baptized with water; but ye shall be baptized with the Holy Ghost not many days hence." Acts 1:5.

5. Was there a similar division in the life of Jesus?

A. Yes. He was born of the Holy Spirit and of Mary and, when He was thirty years of age, the Holy Spirit descended on Him with divine anointing for His ministry.

"And the angel answered and said unto her, The Holy

Ghost shall come upon thee, and the power of the Highest shall overshadow thee: therefore also that holy thing which shall be born of thee shall be called the Son of God." Luke 1:35.

"And I knew him not: but that he shoud be made manifest to Israel, therefore am I come baptizing with water. And John bare record, saying, I saw the Spirit descending from heaven like a dove, and it abode upon him." John 1:31, 32.

6. Was there a similar division in the experience of the apostles?

A. Yes. They had left all to follow Christ, had called Him Lord (by the Holy Spirit), and had their names written in heaven; and later, on the day of Pentecost, they were all filled with the Holy Spirit. Cf. Matthew 19:27; 16:16; Luke 10:20; Acts 2:4.

7. Was there a similar division in the lives of disciples after the outpouring of the Holy Spirit on the Day of Pentecost?

A. Yes. The new converts on that day were told to repent and be baptized and then they would receive the gift of the Holy Spirit. The new converts under Philip at Samaria later received the Holy Spirit under the ministry of Peter and John. And the disciples at Ephesus were baptized in water and then received the Holy Spirit. Cf. Acts 2:38, 39; 8:12, 15, 16; 19:5, 6.

8. What is the promise to believers of all ages with regards to the Holy Spirit?

A. Believers of all ages are promised that they may be filled with the Holy Spirit as the disciples were in the apostolic age.   Cf. Acts 2:38, 39.

9. How may one receive the baptism in the Spirit?

A. One may receive the Baptism in the Spirit by being a Christian in the first place (John 14:17) by asking the Father (Luke 11:13) and by believing on Jesus (John 7:39), and by obeying God. Acts 5:32.

10. How may one know he has been filled with the Spirit?

A. He will speak in other tongues as the Spirit gives him utterance. Cf. Acts 2:4; 10:45, 46; 19:6; 1 Corinthians 14:18.

11. What is the purpose and importance of the baptism in the Holy Spirit?

A. The baptism in the Holy Spirit is primarily enduement with power for witnessing. Since it is the business of the Holy Spirit to convict the world of sin, and since He operates principally in and through believers, it is imperative that the Holy Spirit empower all believers in order to work through them most effectively. Cf. Acts 1:8; Luke 24:47-49.

12. How does the Holy Spirit use those whom He has empowered for service?

A. He imparts to every man certain gifts of the Holy Spirit, "severally as He will."
"But all these worketh that one and the selfsame Spirit, dividing to every man severally as he will." 1 Corinthians 12:11.
"God also bearing them witness, both with signs and wonders, and with divers miracles, and gifts of the Holy Ghost, according to his own will." Hebrews 2:4.

13. Are these gifts described in the Bible?

A. Yes. They are described in 1 Corinthians 12:8-10 and in Romans 12:6-8. Gifts can be classified as gifts of revelation (wisdom, knowledge, and discernment), of power (faith, miracles, and healing), and of utterance (prophecy, tongues and interpretation), as well as other ministries.

14. Are there instructions for the operation of these gifts in the Bible?

A. Yes. 1 Corinthians 14 declares that the purpose of these gifts is to edify the church and that their exercise should be regulated accordingly.

15. What is the relation of these gifts to love and Christian character?

A. While the gifts of the Spirit are important and should be coveted and given proper place in the Church and in Christians' lives, yet love is far more important and must be maintained at all costs. Cf. 1 Corinthians 12:31; 13:1-12; 14:1, 39.

VIII. The Church

1. When was the Church founded?

A. The day of Pentecost immediately following the ascension of Christ was the birthday of the Church. Acts 2.

2. How was the Church founded?

A. The Holy Spirit descended and filled 120 waiting disciples and thus constituted the Church as His abiding place.

"And they were all filled with the Holy Ghost, and began to speak with other tongues, as the Spirit gave them utterance." Acts 2:4.

3. How did the Church grow?

A. The Church grew rapidly by the preaching and teaching of the Word in the power of the Holy Spirit.

"And daily in the temple, and in every house, they

ceased not to teach and preach Jesus Christ." Acts
5:42.

4. What is the nature of the Church?

A. The Holy Spirit is Himself the nature of
the Church. He is refining fire to expose
and punish sin. He is fervent love to bind
the Church together. He is flaming zeal to
carry out the Great Commission. He is divine
power to perform signs and wonders.

5. What is the work and ministry of the Church?

A. The ministry of the Holy Spirit is the ministry of the Church. She must go (under
His impulse and guidance) into all the world.
She must warn every man and make all men
see the beauty of the gospel, and He will
accompany the Word with conviction. She
must teach every man in all wisdom (the
Holy Spirit Himself doing the teaching) and
present every man perfect in Christ Jesus (the
Holy Spirit doing the guiding into all truth.)
"Whom we preach, warning every man, and teaching
every man in all wisdom; that we may present every
man perfect in Christ Jesus: Whereunto I also labour,
striving according to his working, which worketh
in me mightily." Colossians 1:28, 29.
"But ye shall receive power, after that the Holy Ghost
is come upon you: and ye shall be witnesses unto me
both in Jerusalem, and in all Judaea, and in Samaria,
and unto the uttermost part of the earth." Acts 1:8.
Cf. also Matthew 28:19; Mark 16:15.

6. What will be the climax of the ministry of the Church and of the Holy Spirit?

A. This climax will be reached when the Church,
composed of redeemed souls from every kindred, tongue, people and nation is presented
as a chaste virgin to Christ without spot or
wrinkle or any such thing.

"And they sung a new song, saying, Thou art worthy to take the book, and to open the seals thereof: for thou wast slain, and hast redeemed us to God by thy blood out of every kindred, and tongue, and people, and nation." Revelation 5:9.

"For I am jealous over you with godly jealousy: for I have espoused you to one husband, that I may present you as a chaste virgin to Christ." 2 Corinthians 11:2.

"That he might present it to himself a glorious church, not having spot, or wrinkle, or any such thing; but it should be holy and without blemish." Ephesians 5:27.

7. Why should new converts be baptized in water?

A. Jesus commanded it as a public confession of discipleship and a symbol of the death, burial, and resurrection which has taken place in their hearts.

"Go ye therefore, and teach all nations, baptizing them in the name of the Father, and of the Son, and of the Holy Ghost: Teaching them to observe all things whatsoever I have commanded you: and, lo I am with you alway, even unto the end of the world." Matthew 28:19, 20. Cf. also Romans 6:1:5.

8. Which is the correct mode of baptism: sprinkling, pouring, or immersion?

A. Immersion is the correct mode of baptism for it alone is a true picture of the death, burial, and resurrection which it represents.

"What shall we say then? Shall we continue in sin, that grace may abound? God forbid. How shall we, that are dead to sin, live any longer therein? Know ye not, that so many of us as were baptized into Jesus Christ were baptized into his death? Therefore we are buried with him by baptism into death: that like as Christ was raised from the dead by the glory of the Father, even so we also should walk in newness of life. For if we have been planted together in the likeness of his death, we shall be also in the likeness of his resurrection." Romans 6:1-5.

9. Which is the correct formula to be used in baptism?

A. Jesus gave the formula in Matthew 28:19: baptizing them "in the name of the Father, and of the Son, and of the Holy Ghost."

10. Why should believers observe the Lord's supper, or the Holy Communion?

A. Jesus commanded it to be done "in remembrance of me." Cf. 1 Corinthians 11:23-25.

11. What is the significance of this sacred institution?

A. It signifies the broken body and shed blood of our Lord Jesus Christ which we appropriate by faith as we partake of the emblems of that body and blood.

"And when he had given thanks, he brake it, and said, Take, eat: this is my body, which is broken for you: this do in remembrance of me. After the same manner also he took the cup, when he had supped, saying, This cup is the new testament in my blood: this do ye, as oft as ye drink it, in remembrance of me." 1 Corinthians 1:24, 25.

12. Are the emblems actually transformed into the flesh and blood of Christ?

A. No. They simply serve as an object lesson to picture the spiritual blessings which Christ's death gave us.

"For as often as ye eat this bread, and drink this cup, ye do shew the Lord's death till he come." 1 Corinthians 11:26.

13. Is the Communion related to Divine Healing?

A. Yes. The elements of the communion service, the bread and the wine, represent the body of Christ broken for us and His blood (the life of Christ. Cf. Lev. 17:11) poured out for us. By faith as we partake of these emblems we can appropriate the quickening life of Christ for our healing. Isaiah 53:5:

1 Peter 2:24; Matthew 8:17; 1 Corinthians 11:27-30; John 6:51, 55, 56.

14. Who is the Head of the Church?

A. Christ, the Chief Shepherd, is the great head of the Church.

"And hath put all things under his feet, and gave him to be the head over all things to the church." Ephesians 1:22.

15. Who is the head of each local church?

A. The pastor is the head of the local church for Christ has "given unto men . . . pastors" to be His under-shepherds. Cf. 1 Peter 5:1-4.

16. Are there other divinely appointed church officers?

A. Yes. Deacons are ordained of God to assist the pastor, particularly in material matters. Cf. Acts 6:1-6; 1 Timothy 3:8-13.

IX. Spirits

1. Are there invisible beings around us?

A. Yes. When Christ made the world, he created many kinds of beings to worship and serve Him and His Father.

"For by him were all things created, that are in heaven, and that are in earth, visible and invisible, whether they be thrones, or dominions, or principalities, or powers: all things were created by him, and for him." Colossians 1:16.

2. What are the names of these kinds of beings which Christ created?

A. He created cherubim, seraphim, angels, and archangels.

"Above it stood the seraphims: each one had six wings; with twain he covered his face, and with twain he covered his feet, and with twain he did fly." Isaiah 6:2.

"So he drove out the man; and he placed at the east of the garden of Eden Cherubims, and a flaming sword which turned every way, to keep the way of the tree of life." Genesis 3:24.

"Yet Michael the archangel, when contending with the devil he disputed about the body of Moses, durst not bring against him a railing accusation, but said, The Lord rebuke thee." Jude 9.

3. Does the Bible give the individual names of any of these angels?

A. One is Lucifer, created a cherub, and others are Michael the archangel and Gabriel.

"How art thou fallen from heaven, O Lucifer, son of the morning! how art thou cut to the ground, which didst weaken the nations!" Isaiah 14:12.

"Yet Michael the archangel, when contending with the devil, he disputed about the body of Moses, durst not bring against him a railing accusation, but said, The Lord rebuke thee." Jude 9.

"And in the sixth month the angel Gabriel was sent from God unto a city of Galilee, named Nazareth." Luke 1:26.

4. What is the particular record about these beings?

A. Lucifer became proud and rebelled against God and was cast out of heaven to become the devil, or Satan, who is now the "god of this world." Michael is the champion of the Jews and Gabriel is used to take God's special messages to people on the earth.

"Thou art the anointed cherub that covereth; and I have set thee so: thou wast upon the holy mountain of God; thou hast walked up and down in the midst of the stones of fire. Thou wast perfect in thy ways from the day that thou wast created, till iniquity was found in thee." Ezekiel 28:14, 15.

"And at that time shall Michael stand up, the great prince which standeth for the children of thy people; and there shall be a time of trouble, such as never was since there was a nation even to that same time:

and at that time thy people shall be delivered, every one that shall be found written in the book." Daniel 12:1.

"Yea, whiles I was speaking in prayer, even the man Gabriel, whom I had seen in the vision at the beginning, being caused to fly swiftly, touched me about the time of the evening oblation." Daniel 9:21.

5. Was Lucifer the only angel to rebel against God?

A. No. He drew one third of the angels with him and they follow and obey him today.

"And his tail drew the third part of the stars of heaven, and did cast them to the earth: and the dragon stood before the woman which was ready to be delivered, for to devour her child as soon as it was born." Revelation 12:4.

"Then shall he say also unto them on the left hand, Depart from me, ye cursed, into everlasting fire, prepared for the devil and his angels." Matthew 25:41.

6. Are there then good and bad angels?

A. Yes. Good angels are pure. They obey God in ministering to Christians.

"Are they not all ministering spirits, sent forth to minister for them who shall be heirs of salvation?" Hebrews 1:14.

7. What do the bad angels do?

A. There are several kinds of bad angels, or evil spirits. Some are too wicked to be free and God has them bound awaiting their judgment. Others serve Satan in his government of the world. Other evil spirits are called demons who possess very bad people and even animals.

"And the angels which kept not their first estate, but left their own habitation, he hath reserved in everlasting chains under darkness unto the judgment of the great day." Jude 6.

"Then said he, Knowest thou wherefore I come unto thee? and now will I return to fight with the prince of

Persia: and I when I am gone forth, lo, the prince of Grecia shall come." Daniel 10:20.

"And his fame went throughout all Syria: and they brought unto him all sick people that were taken with divers diseases and torments, and those which were possessed with devils, and those which were lunatick, and those that had the palsy; and he healed them." Matthew 4:24.

8. Do Christians need to fear evil spirits?

A. No. As Christians obey God, they have nothing to fear. They can cast out demons by the power and in the name of Jesus.

"And these signs shall follow them that believe; in my name shall they cast out devils; they shall speak with new tongues." Mark 16:17.

9. What will become of angels?

A. Angels never die. The good angels will continue to serve God forever. The evil angels will finally be cast with the devil into hell.

"When the Son of man shall come in his glory, and all the holy angels with him, then shall he sit upon the throne of his glory." Matthew 25:31.

"Then shall he say also unto them on the left hand, Depart from me, ye cursed, into everlasting fire, prepared for the devil and his angels." Matthew 25:41.

X. Prophecy

1. How do we know we are living in the last days?

A. For several reasons:

(1) Some have departed from the faith, giving heed to seducing spirits and doctrines of devils; such as the teachings of Christian Science, Jehovah's Witnesses, Spiritualism, Mormonism, Unity, Theosophy, and Seventh-day Adventism.

"Now the Spirit speaketh expressly, that in the latter times some shall depart from the faith, giving heed to

seducing spirits, and doctrines of devils." 1 Timothy
4:1.

(2) There has been a great falling away with
the denial of the cardinal doctrines of the
Church and the substitution of the theory
of evolution and the worship of man.

"Let no man deceive you by any means: for that day
shall not come, except there come a falling away first,
and that man of sin be revealed, the son of perdition."
2 Thessalonians 2:3.

(3) The Jews have at last returned to Palestine
and are recognized as an independent nation
there, living in a "parted" land.

"And say unto them, Thus saith the Lord God; Behold, I will take the children of Israel from among
the heathen, whither they be gone, and will gather
them on every side, and bring them into their own
land." Ezekiel 37:21.

"I will also gather all nations, and will bring them
down into the valley of Jehoshaphat, and will plead
with them there for my people and for my heritage
Israel, whom they have scattered among the nations,
and *parted my land.*" Joel 3:2.

(4) There is a sort of world government, exist-
ent in the United Nations preliminary to the
Federation of Nations over which the Antichrist is to rule.

"And it was given unto him to make war with the
saints, and to overcome them: and power was given
him over all kindreds, and tongues, and nations."
Revelation 13:7.

(5) The world now has the means of working
the destruction of half of mankind as predicted in Revelation 6:8 and 9:18.

"And I looked, and behold a pale horse: and his name
that sat on him was Death, and Hell followed with
him. And power was given unto them over the fourth

part of the earth, to kill with sword, and with hunger, and with death, and with the beasts of the earth." Revelation 6:8.

"By these three was the third part of men killed, by the fire, and by the smoke, and by the brimstone, which issued out of their mouths." Revelation 9:18.

2. What do these conditions tell us is just ahead in world history?

A. Just ahead is the Great Tribulation which Jesus said would come on the earth; in which, except those days should be shortened, there should no flesh be saved.

"For then shall be great tribulation, such as was not since the beginning of the world to this time, no, nor ever shall be." Matthew 24:21. Cf. also Daniel 12:1; Jeremiah 30:4-9.

3. What is the duty of the Church in these days?

A. It is the Church's duty to warn the world of approaching judgment and proclaim the soon coming of Jesus, and to preach the gospel of God's grace in Christ.

"Whom we preach, warning every man, and teaching every man in all wisdom; that we may present every man perfect in Christ Jesus." Colossians 1:28.

"And at midnight there was a cry made, Behold, the bridegroom cometh; go ye out to meet him." Matthew 25:6.

4. Will Christians go into the Great Tribulation?

A. No. The Lord has promised to spare them from that distress.

"And they shall be mine, saith the Lord of hosts, in that day when I make up my jewels; and I will spare them, as a man spareth his own son that serveth him." Malachi 3:17.

"For God hath not appointed us to wrath, but to obtain salvation by your Lord Jesus Christ." 1 Thessalonians 5:9.

"Because thou hast kept the word of my patience, I also will keep thee from the hour of temptation, which shall come upon all the world, to try them that dwell upon the earth." Revelation 3:10.

"The Lord knoweth how to deliver the godly out of temptations, and to reserve the unjust unto the day of judgment to be punished." 2 Peter 2:9.

5. How will they escape?

A. The Lord will descend from heaven in the clouds and catch away all those who are "in Christ," both living and dead.

"Behold, I shew you a mystery; We shall not all sleep, but we shall all be changed, in a moment, in a twinkling of an eye, at the last trump: for the trumpet shall sound, and the dead shall be raised incorruptible, and we shall be changed. For this corruptible must put on incorruption, and this mortal must put on immortality." 1 Corinthians 15:51-53.

"For the Lord himself shall descend from heaven with a shout, with the voice of the archangel, and with the trump of God: and the dead in Christ shall rise first: Then we which are alive and remain shall be caught up together with them in the clouds, to meet the Lord in the air: and so shall we ever be with the Lord." 1 Thessalonians 4:16-17.

6. What is this glorious event called?

A. It is called the Rapture of the Saints, which describes the experience, although the word "rapture" is not found in the New Testament.

7. Has anyone ever gone to heaven without dying?

A. Only Enoch and Elijah.

"By faith Enoch was translated that he should not see death; and was not found, because God had translated him: for before his translation he had this testimony, that he pleased God." Hebrews 11:5.

"And it came to pass, as they still went on, and talked, that, behold, there appeared a chariot of fire, and horses of fire, and parted them both asunder; and Elijah went up by a whirlwind into heaven." 2 Kings 2:11.

8. What is the Bema Judgment?

A. It is the judgment of Christians which will take place in the heavenlies just after the resurrection and rapture of the saints at the end of the age.

"But why dost thou judge thy brother? or why dost thou set at nought thy brother? for we shall all stand before the judgment seat of Christ." Romans 14:10.

9. Why and how will Christians be judged?

A. Justice demands that Christians be judged in order to give them fair reward for their varying degrees of consecration and faithfulness. They will be judged according to the deeds done in the flesh, whether they be good or bad.

"For we must all appear before the judgment seat of Christ; that every one may receive the things done in his body, according to that he hath done, whether it be good or bad." 2 Corinthians 5:10. Cf. also 1 Corinthians 3:10-15.

10. What is the "Marriage Supper of the Lamb"?

A. The Marriage Supper of the Lamb is the great celebration in heaven toward the end of the tribulation when Christ and all His redeemed eat and drink together in the kingdom of God.

"That ye may eat and drink at my table in my kingdom, and sit on thrones judging the twelve tribes of Israel." Luke 22:30. Cf. also Revelation 19:7-9.

"But I say unto you, I will not drink henceforth of this fruit of the vine, until that day when I drink it new with you in my Father's kingdom." Matthew 26:29.

11. What is the "Battle of Armageddon"?

A. It is the last great battle of this dispensation when the Antichrist and all the armies of the world are gathered together to fight

against the Lord Jesus Christ. The Lord
shall come forth from heaven riding on a
white horse with the armies of heaven on
white horses.

"And he gathered them together into a place called in
the Hebrew tongue Armageddon." Revelation 16:16.
"And I saw heaven opened, and behold a white horse;
and he that sat upon him was called Faithful and True,
and in righteousness he doth judge and make war."
Revelation 19:11.
"And I saw the beast, and the kings of the earth, and
their armies, gathered to make war against him that
sat on the horse, and against his army." Revelation
19:19.

12. What will be the result of this battle?

A. The Antichrist and the false prophet (his
religious leader) will be taken alive and cast
into the lake of fire and all the soldiers of
his armies will be slain. Jesus and His armies
(the glorified saints) will take over the
government of this world.

"And the beast was taken, and with him the false
prophet that wrought miracles before him, with which
he deceived them that had received the mark of the
beast, and them that worshipped his image. These
both were cast alive into a lake of fire burning with
brimstone. And the remnant were slain with the
sword of him that sat upon the horse, which sword
proceeded out of his mouth: and all the fowls were
filled with their flesh." Revelation 19:20, 21.

"And Enoch also, the seventh from Adam, prophesied
of these, saying, Behold, the Lord cometh with ten
thousands of his saints." Jude 14.

13. What is the "Judgment of the Living Nations"?

A. When Jesus comes and sits upon the throne
of His glory in Palestine, representatives of all
nations will be gathered before Him and He

will judge and classify them in accordance to their treatment of His people, the Jews (who then will have accepted Him as their Messiah). Those who have been kind to the Jews will be allowed to continue on intact into His reign, but those who have been unkind to the Jews will be dissolved as nations and their leaders (those responsible for the mistreatment of the Jews) will be assigned to hell.

"When the Son of man shall come in his glory, and all the holy angels with him, then shall he sit upon the throne of his glory: And before him shall be gathered all nations: and he shall separate them one from another, as a shepherd divideth his sheep from the goats: And he shall set the sheep on his right hand, but the goats on the left.

"Then shall the King say unto them on his right hand, Come, ye blessed of my Father, inherit the kingdom prepared for you from the foundation of the world: For I was an hungred, and ye gave me meat; I was thirsty, and ye gave me drink: I was a stranger, and ye took me in: Naked, and ye clothed me: I was sick, and ye visited me; I was in prison, and ye came unto me.

"Then shall the righteous answer him saying, Lord, when saw we thee an hungred, and fed thee? or thirsty, and gave thee drink? When saw we thee a stranger, and took thee in? or naked, and clothed thee? Or when saw we thee sick, or in prison, and came unto thee? "And the King shall answer and say unto them: Verily I say unto you, inasmuch as ye have done it unto one of the least of these my brethren, ye have done it unto me.

"Then shall he say also unto them on the left hand, Depart from me, ye cursed, into everlasting fire, prepared for the devil and his angels: For I was an hungred, and ye gave me no meat: I was thirsty, and ye gave me no drink: I was a stranger, and ye took me not in: naked, and ye clothed me not: sick, and in prison, and ye visited me not.

"Then shall they also answer him, saying, Lord, when saw we thee an hungred, or thirsty, or a stranger or naked, or sick, or in prison, and did not minister unto thee?

"Then shall he answer them, saying, Verily I say unto you, Inasmuch as ye did it not to one of the least of these, ye did it not to me. And these shall go away into everlasting punishment: but the righteous into life eternal." Matthew 25:31-46.

14. What will follow this Judgment?

A. Jesus will establish a righteous government on the earth and there will be peace in all the world for one thousand years. A temple will be built in Palestine which will be the religious center of the world and the Jews will be the leading nation of the earth. The curse will be lifted from nature and wild animals will be tame.

"And I saw thrones, and they sat upon them, and judgment was given unto them: and I saw the souls of them that were beheaded for the witness of Jesus, and for the word of God, and which had not worshiped the beast, neither his image, neither had received his mark upon their foreheads, or in their hands; and they lived and reigned with Christ a thousand years." Revelation 20:4.

"And many people shall go and say, Come ye, and let us go up to the mountain of the Lord, to the house of the God of Jacob; and he will teach us of his ways, and we will walk in his paths: for out of Zion shall go forth the law, and the word of the Lord from Jerusalem." Isaiah 2:3.

"The wolf also shall dwell with the lamb, and the leopard shall lie down with the calf and the young lion and the fatling together; and a little child shall lead them. And the cow and the bear shall feed; their young ones shall lie down together: and the lion shall eat straw like the ox." Isaiah 11:6, 7.

"The wolf and the lamb shall feed together, and the lion shall eat straw like the bullock: and dust shall be the serpent's meat. They shall not hurt nor destroy in all my holy mountain, saith the Lord." Isaiah 65:25.

15. What event will mark the end of time?

A. The Great White Throne Judgment. At the end of the Millennium (the 1,000 years of peace) the devil will be released from the bottomless pit (where he will have been bound right after Armageddon). God will gather out of His kingdom everything that offends, and He will burn them up with fire from heaven. The devil will be confined forever in the Lake of Fire. Then God will call all the wicked dead to judgment and assign them their place in hell according as their works shall deserve. He will purify His whole world by fire and prepare it for eternity. The New Jerusalem will then come down from God out of heaven and God will live and reign with and over His people for ever and ever.

"And when the thousand years are expired, Satan shall be loosed out of his prison. And the devil that deceived them was cast into the lake of fire and brimstone, where the beast and the false prophet are, and shall be tormented day and night for ever and ever." Revelation 20:7, 10.

"And I saw a great white throne, and him that sat on it, from whose face the earth and the heaven fled away; and there was found no place for them. And whosoever was not found written in the book of life was cast into the lake of fire." Revelation 20:11, 15. "But the day of the Lord will come as a thief in the night; in the which the heavens shall pass away with a great noise, and the elements shall melt with fervent heat, the earth also and the works that are therein shall be burned up." 2 Peter 3:10.

"And I John saw the holy city, new Jerusalem, coming down from God out of heaven, prepared as a bride adorned for her husband. And I heard a great voice out of heaven saying, Behold, the tabernacle of God is with men, and he will dwell with them, and they shall be his people, and God himself shall be with them, and be their God." Revelation 21:2, 3.

"And there shall be no night there; and they need no candle, neither light of the sun; for the Lord God giveth them light: and they shall reign for ever and ever." Revelation 22:5.

PART 4
Christian Living, Bible Book Studies for Adults

A. CHRISTIAN LIVING

I. New Testament Commandments

1. Are Christians under the law or under grace?

A. Christians are not under the Old Testament law but are saved and kept by grace through faith.

"For by grace are ye saved through faith; and that not of yourselves: it is the gift of God." Ephesians 2:8.

"Who are kept by the power of God through faith unto salvation ready to be revealed in the last time." 1 Peter 1:5.

2. Does this free Christians from keeping the Old Testament law?

A. Yes, except where that law is repeated in the New Testament.

"For sin shall not have dominion over you: for ye are not under the law, but under grace." Romans 6:14.

3. Since Christians are saved by grace, are they not therefore free from all commandments?

A. No. They are "under the law to Christ."

"To them that are without law, as without law (being not without law to God, but under the law to Christ,) that I might gain them that are without law." 1 Corinthians 9:21.

4. What did Jesus Himself say about this?

A. "If ye love me, keep my commandments." John 14:15. "He that hath my commandments and keepeth them, he it is that loveth me." John 14:21.

5. Are there other New Testament statements about keeping commandments?

A. Yes.

"And whatsoever we ask, we receive of him, because we keep his commandments, and do those things that are pleasing in his sight. And this is his commandment, That we should believe on the name of his Son Jesus Christ, and love one another, as he gave us

135

commandment. And he that keepeth his commandments dwelleth in him, and he in him. And hereby we know that he abideth in us, by the Spirit which he hath given us." 1 John 3:22-24.

"By this we know that we love the children of God, when we love God, and keep his commandments." 1 John 5:2.

"For this is the love of God, that we keep his commandments: and his commandments are not grievous." 1 John 5:3.

"If ye fulfill the royal law according to the scripture, Thou shalt love thy neighbor as thy self, ye do well: But if ye have respect to persons, ye commit sin, and are convinced of the law as transgressors. For whosoever shall keep the whole law, and yet offend in one point, he is guilty of all. For he that said, Do not commit adultery, said also, Do not kill. Now if thou commit no adultery, yet if thou kill, thou art become a transgressor of the law. So speak ye, and so do, as they that shall be judged by the law of liberty." James 2:8-12.

"Blessed are they that do his commandments, that they may have right to the tree of life, and may enter in through the gates into the city." Revelation 22:14. "Circumcision is nothing, and uncircumcision is nothing, but the keeping of the commandments of God." 1 Corinthians 7:19.

6. Are there not many New Testament scriptures which release us from keeping the law?

A. Yes.

"But he is a Jew, which is one inwardly; and circumcision is that of the heart, in the spirit, and not in the letter; whose praise is not of men, but of God." Romans 2:29.

"Therefore by the deeds of the law there shall no flesh be justified in his sight: for by the law is the knowledge of sin. Therefore we conclude that a man is justified by faith without the deeds of the law." Romans 3:20, 28.

"And if by grace, then is it no more of works: otherwise grace is no more grace. But if it be of works, then is it no more grace: otherwise work is no more work." Romans 11:6.

"For he that loveth another hath fulfilled the law. Therefore love is the fulfilling of the law." Romans 13:8b, 10b.

"But that no man is justified by the law in the sight of God, it is evident: for, The just shall live by faith. And the law is not of faith: but, The man that doeth them shall live in them." Galatians 3:11, 12.

"Christ is become of no effect unto you, whosoever of you are justified by the law; ye are fallen from grace. But if ye be led of the Spirit, ye are not under the law." Galatians 5:4, 18.

"But if the ministration of death, written and engraven in stones, was glorious, so that the children of Israel could not stedfastly behold the face of Moses for the glory of his countenance; which glory was to be done away." 2 Corinthians 3:7.

"For there is verily a disannulling of the commandment going before for the weakness and unprofitableness thereof." "In that he saith, a new covenant, he hath made the first old. Now that which decayeth and waxeth old is ready to vanish away." Hebrews 7:18; 8:13.

7. How are all these scriptures reconciled and harmonized?

A. These things are eternally true:

(1) Doing good things by one's own strength produces self-righteousness and is filthy rags in His sight.

"But we are all as an unclean thing, and all our righteousnesses are as filthy rags; and we all do fade as a leaf; and our iniquities, like the wind, have taken us away." Isaiah 64:6.

"And be found in him, not having mine own righteousness, which is of the law, but that which is through the faith of Christ, the righteousness which is of God by faith." Philippians 3:9.

(2) No man is sinless before God and all are in need of His mercy and grace.

"If we say that we have no sin, we deceive ourselves, and the truth is not in us." 1 John 1:8.

(3) His boundless grace and power with which to do good are available to all who confess sin and need, and who accept Jesus as their Saviour.

"According as his divine power hath given unto us all things that pertain unto life and godliness, through the knowledge of him that hath called us to glory and virtue." 2 Peter 1:3.

(4) Right is forever right and righteousness is still righteousness and His grace is given "That the righteousness of the law might be fulfilled in us, who walk not after the flesh, but after the Spirit." Romans 8:4.

(5) The New Testament abounds with descriptions of righteousness as applicable to Christians who are "under grace."

"And be ye kind one to another, tenderhearted, forgiving one another, even as God for Christ's sake hath forgiven you." Ephesians 4:32.

"Put on therefore, as the elect of God, holy and beloved, bowels of mercies, kindness, humbleness of mind, meekness, longsuffering; forbearing one another, and forgiving one another, if any man have a quarrel against any: even as Christ forgave you, so do ye. And above all these things put on charity, which is the bond of perfectness." Colossians 3:12-14.

(6) These scriptures demand that New Testament Christians keep New Testament commandments and live holy, righteous lives.

"Thy throne, O God, is for ever and ever: a sceptre of righteousness is the sceptre of thy kingdom." Hebrews 1:8.

"But as he which hath called you is holy, so be ye holy in all manner of conversation; because it is written, Be ye holy; for I am holy." 1 Peter 1:15, 16.

"Follow peace with all men, and holiness, without

which no man shall see the Lord." Hebrews 12:14.

(7) Therefore God demands that His grace be appropriated and manifested in Christians' lives, producing godliness and holiness in terms of obedience to all New Testament commandments.

"We then, as workers together with him, beseech you also that ye receive not the grace of God in vain. Having therefore these promises, dearly beloved, let us cleanse ourselves from all filthiness of the flesh and spirit, perfecting holiness in the fear of God." 2 Corinthians 6:1; 7:1.

II. Duties to God

1. What is our first duty to God?

A. "Thou shalt love the Lord thy God with all thy heart, and with all thy soul, and with all thy mind. This is the first and great commandment." Matthew 22:37, 38.

2. What does this mean?

A. It is expressed negatively in the Old Testament: "Thou shalt have no other gods before me." Exodus 20:3. God must be first in our affections, and every other object of our affections must be held in second place to God. All our cherished possessions must be on His altar continually.

3. What will this mean in the lives of Christians?

A. Obedience to this commandment will mean placing at God's disposal one's family, one's possessions, and one's own entire life.

"Then said Jesus unto his disciples, If any man will come after me, let him deny himself, and take up his cross, and follow me. For whosoever will save his life shall lose it: and whosoever will lose his life for my sake shall find it." Matthew 16:24, 25.

4. Does God really require all this?

A. He requires not one whit less.

"I beseech you therefore, brethren, by the mercies of God, that ye present your bodies a living sacrifice, holy, acceptable unto God, which is your reasonable service." Romans 12:1.

"So likewise, whosoever he be of you that forsaketh not all that he hath, he cannot be my disciple." Luke 14:33.

5. What other duty is there which we have to God?

A. We must worship Him.

"Thou shalt worship the Lord thy God and Him only shalt thou serve." Matthew 4:10.

"God is a Spirit: and they that worship him must worship him in spirit and in truth. The Father seeketh such to worship Him." John 4:24, 23.

6. What does this mean?

A. To worship is to express affection, respect and adoration. God is the only legitimate object of the soul's worship and He seeks and requires our worship. Such exercise is also good and wholesome for our souls. John 4:23, 24.

7. Is there another duty to God?

A. Yes. We should glorify Him with our mind and our mouth, in our body and in our spirit, which are God's.

"That ye may with one mind and one mouth glorify God, even the Father of our Lord Jesus Christ." Romans 15:6.

"For ye are bought with a price: therefore glorify God in your body, and in your spirit, which are God's. 1 Corinthians 6:20.

8. How can we glorify God?

A. We can glorify God by praising Him with our lips, by our good works, and by bearing much fruit for His glory.

"Ye that fear the Lord, praise him; all ye the seed of

Jacob, glorify him; and fear him, all ye the seed of
Israel." Psalm 22:23.

"Let your light so shine before men, that they may
see your good works, and glorify your Father which is
in heaven." Matthew 5:16.

"Herein is my Father glorified, that ye bear much
fruit; so shall ye be my disciples." John 15:8.

III. Duties to the Church

1. What is a Christian's first duty to the church?

A. A Christian's first duty to the church is to
belong to it.

"And the Lord added to the church daily such as
should be saved." Acts 2:47.

"And believers were the more added to the Lord,
multitudes both of men and women." Acts 5:14.

"And the word of God increased; and the number of
the disciples multiplied in Jerusalem greatly; and a
great company of the priests were obedient to the
faith." Acts 6:7.

2. Are not all born-again Christians automatically members of the body of Christ?

A. Yes.

"By one Spirit are we all baptized into one body,
whether we be Jews or Gentiles, whether we be bond
or free; and have been all made to drink into one
Spirit." 1 Corinthians 12:13.

3. Why then is it necessary for new converts to "join" a church?

A. Joining a church, like water baptism, is an
outward expression of an inward act. The
Holy Ghost "joins" the new convert to Christ
as a branch is grafted into a vine. This is
done in the Spirit and is recorded in heaven.
But the new convert must acknowledge that
this spiritual work has been done and must
not repudiate it. "That if thou shalt confess
with thy mouth the Lord Jesus, and shalt
believe in thine heart that God hath raised

him from the dead, thou shalt be saved. For with the heart man believeth unto righteousness; and with the mouth confession is made unto salvation." Romans 10:9, 10. The faith in the heart must be confessed with the mouth to make the salvation complete. A new Christian should likewise confirm in a visible and outward way what has taken place in his heart and in heaven.

4. Is there another reason why a new Christian should join a church?

A. Yes. He is now a member of the family of God and naturally should seek fellowship among his brothers and sisters in the Lord. "We know that we have passed from death unto life, because we love the brethren. He that loveth not his brother abideth in death." 1 John 3:14.

5. What advantages are there in belonging to a church?

A. There are many:

(1) One thus receives regular ministry of the Word of God.

(2) One has more opportunities for Christian service.

(3) One has the privilege of collective worship with other members of the Body of Christ.

(4) One can here pool his efforts and his contributions for more effective results.

(5) One can receive personal assistance in time of need of any kind.

(6) And one has the joy of spiritual companionship with those of similar faith and experience.

6. After joining a church, what is a Christian's duty to that church?

A. That duty is manifold:

(1) He should conduct himself in a way which will reflect credit rather than blame on his church.

"Give none offence, neither to the Jews, nor to the Gentiles, nor to the church of God." 1 Corinthians 10:32. Cf. 1 Peter 2:12.

(2) He should attend as many of its services as possible in order to gain fully the advantage of his membership there.

"Not forsaking the assembling of ourselves together, as the manner of some is; but exhorting one another: and so much the more, as ye see the day approaching." Hebrew 10:25.

(3) He should respect and be loyal to the pastor of his church.

"Obey them that have the rule over you, and submit yourselves: for they watch for your souls, as they that must give account, that they may do it with joy, and not with grief: for that is unprofitable for you." Hebrews 13:17.

"And we beseech you, brethren, to know them which labour among you, and are over you in the Lord, and admonish you; and to esteem them very highly in love for their work's sake. And be at peace among yourselves." 1 Thessalonians 5:12, 13.

(4) He should pay his tithes and offerings into that church.

"Bring ye all the tithes into the storehouse, that there may be meat in mine house, and prove me now herewith, saith the Lord of hosts, if I will not open you the windows of heaven, and pour you out a blessing, that there shall not be room enough to receive it." Malachi 3:10.

"Now concerning the collection for the saints, as I have given order to the churches of Galatia, even so do ye. Upon the first day of the week let every one of you lay by him in store, as God hath prospered

him, that there be no gatherings when I come." 1
Corinthians 16:1, 2.

"Moreover, brethren, we do you to wit of the grace of
God bestowed on the churches of Macedonia; how
that in a great trial of affliction the abundance of their
joy and their deep poverty abounded unto the riches
of their liberality. For to their power, I bear record,
yea, and beyond their power they were willing of
themselves; praying us with much intreaty that we
would receive the gift, and take upon us the fellowship of the ministering to the saints." 2 Corinthians
8:1-4.

(5) He should participate in the program of that
church to the full extent of his ability.

"As every man hath received the gift, even so minister
the same one to another, as good stewards of the manifold grace of God. If any man speak, let him speak
as the oracles of God; if any man minister, let him
do it as of the ability which God giveth: that God in
all things may be glorified through Jesus Christ, to
whom be praise and dominion for ever and ever." 1
Peter 4:10, 11.

"Having then gifts differing according to the grace
that is given to us, whether prophecy, let us prophesy
according to the proportion of faith; or ministry, let
us wait on our ministering: or he that teacheth, on
teaching; or he that exhorteth, on exhortation: he
that giveth, let him do it with simplicity; he that
ruleth, with diligence; he that sheweth mercy, with
cheerfulness." Romans 12:6-8.

IV. Duties to Christians

1. What is the chief duty of one Christian to another?

A. His first and foremost duty is to love his
brother.

"A new commandment I give unto you, That ye love
one another; as I have loved you, that ye also love
one another. By this shall all men know that ye are
my disciples, if ye have love one to another." John
13:34, 35.

"Seeing ye have purified your souls in obeying the truth through the Spirit unto unfeigned love of the brethren, see that ye love one another with a pure heart fervently." 1 Peter 1:22.

2. How should this love be expressed?

A. This love should be expressed not merely in words but in deeds.

"But whoso hath this world's good, and seeth his brother have need, and shutteth up his bowels of compassion from him, how dwelleth the love of God in him? My little children, let us not love in word, neither in tongue; but in deed and in truth." 1 John 3:17, 18.

3. What are some of the deeds of love which a Christian performs for, or toward, his brother?

A. (1) To be kind and tenderhearted.

"And be ye kind one to another, tenderhearted, forgiving one another, even as God for Christ's sake hath forgiven you." Ephesians 4:32.

(2) To forbear and forgive.

"Forbearing one another, and forgiving one another, if any man have a quarrel against any: even as Christ forgave you, so also do ye." Colossians 3:13.

"So likewise shall my heavenly Father do also unto you, if ye from your hearts forgive not every one his brother their trespasses." Matthew 18:35.

(3) To esteem other better than himself.

"Let nothing be done through strife or vainglory; but in lowliness of mind let each esteem other better than themselves." Philippians 2:3.

(4) To serve.

"For, brethren, ye have been called unto liberty; only use not liberty for an occasion to the flesh, but by love serve one another." Galatians 5:13.

"Let no man seek his own, but every man another's wealth." 1 Corinthians 10:24.

(5) To teach and admonish.

"Let the word of Christ dwell in you richly in all wisdom; teaching and admonishing one another in psalms and hymns and spiritual songs, singing with grace in your hearts to the Lord." Colossians 3:16.

(6) To submit to one another.

"Submitting yourselves one to another in the fear of God." Ephesians 5:21.

(7) To confess his faults to and pray for his brother.

"Confess your faults one to another, and pray one for another, that ye may be healed. The effectual fervent prayer of a righteous man availeth much." James 5:16.

(8) To assist materially as needed.

"If a brother or sister be naked, and destitute of daily food, and one of you say unto them, Depart in peace, be ye warmed and filled; notwithstanding ye give them not those things which are needful to the body; what doth it profit?" James 2:15-16.

4. Disobedience to which of the above brings serious consequences?

A. If we do not forgive our brethren, our heavenly Father will not forgive us. This declaration of Christ is given in connection with the Lord's prayer and is also emphasized by Him in a lengthy parable.

"But if ye forgive not men their trespasses, neither will your Father forgive your trespasses." Matthew 6:15.

"Then came Peter to him, and said, Lord, how oft shall my brother sin against me, and I forgive him? till seven times? Jesus saith unto him, I say not unto thee, Until seven times: but, Until seventy times seven.

"Therefore is the kingdom of heaven likened unto a certain king, which would take account of his servants. And when he had begun to reckon, one was brought unto him, which owed him ten thousand talents. But forasmuch as he had not to pay, his lord commanded him to be sold, and his wife, and children, and all that he had, and payment to be made. The servant therefore fell down, and worshipped him, saying, Lord, have patience with me, and I will pay thee all. Then the lord of that servant was moved with compassion, and loosed him, and forgave him the debt. But the same servant went out, and found one of his fellowservants, which owed him an hundred pence: and he laid hands on him, and took him by the throat, saying, Pay me that thou owest. And his fellowservant fell down at his feet, and besought him saying, Have patience with me, and I will pay thee all. And he would not: but went and cast him into prison, till he should pay the debt. So when his fellowservants saw what was done, they were very sorry, and came and told unto their lord all that was done.

"Then his lord, after that he had called him, said unto him, O thou wicked servant, I forgave thee all that debt, because thou desiredst me: shouldest not thou also have compassion on thy fellowservant, even as I had pity on thee? And his lord was wroth, and delivered him to the tormentors, till he should pay all that was due unto him. So likewise shall my heavenly Father do also unto you, if ye from your hearts forgive not every one his brother their trespasses." Matthew 18:21-35.

5. Are there particular instructions concerning weaker and stronger brothers?

A. Yes. They that are strong are told to bear the infirmites of the weak and not to please themselves. The strong must not look down upon the weak and the weak must not criticize the strong. The strong must deny themselves any practices which stumble their weaker brethren.

"Him that is weak in the faith receive ye, but not to doubtful disputations. For one believeth that he may eat all things: another, who is weak, eateth herbs. Let not him that eateth despise him that eateth not; and

let not him which eateth not judge him that eateth:
for God hath received him.

"Who art thou that judgest another man's servant?
to his own master he standeth or falleth. Yea, he shall
be holden up: for God is able to make him stand.

"One man esteemeth one day above another: another
esteemeth every day alike. Let every man be fully
persuaded in his own mind. He that regardeth the day,
regardeth it unto the Lord; and he that regardeth not
the day, to the Lord he doth not regard it.

"He that eateth, eateth to the Lord, that he giveth
God thanks; and he that eateth not, to the Lord he
eateth not, and giveth God thanks.

"For none of us liveth to himself, and no man dieth
to himself. For whether we live, we live unto the
Lord; and whether we die, we die unto the Lord:
whether we live therefore, or die, we are the Lord's.
For to this end Christ both died, and rose, and revived,
that he might be Lord both of the dead and living.
But why dost thou judge thy brother? or why dost
thou set at nought thy brother? for we shall all stand
before the judgment seat of Christ. For it is written,
As I live, saith the Lord, every knee shall bow to me,
and every tongue shall confess to God. So then every
one of us shall give account of himself to God. Let
us not therefore judge one another any more: but
judge this rather, that no man put a stumblingblock
or an occasion to fall in his brother's way.

"I know, and am persuaded by the Lord Jesus, that
there is nothing unclean of itself: but to him that
esteemeth any thing to be unclean, to him it is unclean. But if thy brother be grieved with thy meat, now
walkest thou not charitably. Destroy not him with thy
meat, for whom Christ died. Let not then your good be
evil spoken of: For the kingdom of God is not meat
and drink; but righteousness, and peace, and joy in
the Holy Ghost. For he that in these things serveth
Christ is acceptable to God, and approved of men.
"Let us therefore follow after the things which make
for peace, and things wherewith one may edify another. For meat destroy not the work of God. All
things indeed are pure; but it is evil for that man

who eateth with offence. It is good neither to eat
flesh, nor to drink wine, nor any thing whereby thy
brother stumbleth, or is offended, or is made weak.
Hast thou faith? have it to thyself before God. Happy
is he that condemneth not himself in that thing which
he alloweth. And he that doubteth is damned if he eat,
because he eateth not of faith: for whatsoever is not
of faith is sin.

"We then that are strong ought to bear the infirmities
of the weak, and not to please ourselves. Let every
one of us please his neighbour for his good to edification. For even Christ pleased not himself; but, as it
is written, The reproaches of them that reproached
thee fell on me. For whatsoever things were written
aforetime were written for our learning, that we
through patience and comfort of the scriptures might
have hope." Romans 14:1-15:4.

V. Duties to Parents

1. What is the fifth commandment?

A. "Honor thy father and thy mother: that thy
days may be long upon the land which the
Lord thy God giveth thee." Exodus 20:12.

2. Is this commandment renewed in the New Testament?

A. Yes.

"Children, obey your parents in the Lord: for this is
right. Honour thy father and mother: which is
the first commandment with promise; that it may be
well with thee, and thou mayest live long on the
earth." Ephesians 6:1-3.

"Children, obey your parents in all things: for this
is well pleasing unto the Lord." Colossians 3:20.

3. May we give to God that which we owe to our parents?

A. No. Jesus rebuked the Pharisees for approv-
ing that practice.

"And he said unto them, Full well ye reject the
commandment of God, that ye may keep your own
tradition. For Moses said, Honour thy father and
thy mother; and, Whoso curseth father or mother, let
him die the death: but ye say, If a man shall say to
his father or mother, It is Corban, that is to say, a gift,

by whatsoever thou mightest be profited by me; he shall be free. And ye suffer him no more to do ought for his father or mother; making the word of God of none effect through your tradition, which ye have delivered: and many such like things do ye." Mark 7:9-13.

4. Shall we love and obey our parents more than we love and obey God?

A. No. And we are to obey our parents only "in the Lord."

"He that loveth father or mother more than me is not worthy of me." Matthew 10:37.
"Children, obey your parents in the Lord: for this is right." Ephesians 6:1.

5. Give the Bible example of perfect childhood.

A. Jesus was the example of perfect childhood. He was subject to His parents and as He increased in stature He increased in wisdom and in favor with God and man. He waxed strong in spirit, filled with wisdom; and the grace of God was upon Him.

"And the child grew, and waxed strong in spirit, filled with wisdom: and the grace of God was upon him. And he went down with them, and came to Nazareth, and was subject unto them: but his mother kept all these sayings in her heart. And Jesus increased in wisdom and stature, and in favour with God and man." Luke 2:40, 51-52.

VI. Duties to Wives and Husbands

1. Why is the relationship between husband and wife especially emphasized in the New Testament?

A. Because it is an illustration and an example of the relationship which exists between Christ and His church.

"For the husband is the head of the wife, even as Christ is the head of the church: and he is the saviour of the body. Therefore as the church is subject unto Christ, so let the wives be to their own husbands in every thing. Husbands, love your wives, even as Christ also loved the church, and gave himself for it; that he might sanctify and cleanse it with the washing of water by the word, that he might present it to himself a glorious church, not having spot, or wrinkle, or any such thing; but that it should be holy and without blemish. So ought men to love their wives as their own bodies. He that loveth his wife loveth himself. For no man ever yet hated his own flesh; but nourisheth and cherisheth it, even as the Lord the church. For we are members of his body, of his flesh, and of his bones. For this cause shall a man leave his father and mother, and shall be joined unto his wife, and they two shall be one flesh. This is a great mystery: but I speak concerning Christ and the church. Nevertheless let every one of you in particular so love his wife even as himself; and the wife see that she reverence her husband." Ephesians 5:23-33.

2. Of what other spiritual relationship is it illustrative?

A. It is also illustrative of the Spirit-filled life. "Submitting yourselves one to another in the fear of God. Wives, submit yourselves unto your own husbands, as unto the Lord." Ephesians 5:21-22.

3. How is married life similar to the Spirit-filled life?

A. Spirit-filled Christians submit themselves one to another and love each other as a wife submits herself to her husband and as he loves his wife.

"Submitting yourselves one to another in the fear of God. Wives, submit yourselves unto your own husbands, as unto the Lord. Husbands, love your wives, even as Christ also loved the church, and gave himself for it." Ephesians 5:21, 22, 25.

4. What is the duty of a man to his wife?

A. His first duty is to leave his father and mother and cleave unto his wife.

"For this cause shall a man leave his father and mother,

and shall be joined unto his wife, and they two shall be one flesh." Ephesians 5:31.

"And he answered and said unto them, Have ye not read, that he which made them at the beginning made them male and female, and said, For this cause shall a man leave father and mother, and shall cleave to his wife: and they twain shall be one flesh?" Matthew 19:4-5.

5. What does this imply?

A. This implies that a man's wife should have his consideration above his parents, and that it is best for a young couple to live by themselves.

6. What is a man's chief duty to his wife?

A. He should love and cherish his wife, even as he does his own body.

"So ought men to love their wives as their own bodies. He that loveth his wife loveth himself. For no man ever yet hated his own flesh; but nourisheth and cherisheth it, even as the Lord the church." Ephesians 5:28-29.

7. What does this involve?

A. It involves his "forsaking all others" and keeping only unto her as long as they both shall live.   It includes providing for her and their children to the extent of his ability and it also calls for his tender consideration of her under all circumstances.

"But if any provide not for his own, and specially for those of his own house, he hath denied the faith, and is worse than an infidel." 1 Timothy 5:8.

8. Will his love for his wife properly lead him to make the will and call of God secondary to her wishes?

A. No. The wife is included in the list of family relationships that are specifically placed subordinate to Christ.

"If any man come to me, and hate not his father, and mother, and wife, and children, and brethren, and sisters, yea, and his own life also, he cannot be my disciple." Luke 14:26.

"And he said unto them, Verily I say unto you, There is no man that hath left house, or parents, or brethren, or wife, or children, for the kingdom of God's sake." Luke 18:29.

9. What well-known Bible character made his wife's wishes more important than the command of God, and with what result?

A. Adam was not deceived when he ate of the forbidden fruit but deliberately accepted it at his wife's hands. The result was the fall of the human race and its attendant calamities.

"And Adam was not deceived, but the woman being deceived was in the transgression." 1 Timothy 2:14.

10. What is a woman's duty to her husband?

A. It is her duty to reverence her own husband and be in subjection to him.

"Therefore as the church is subject unto Christ, so let the wives be to their own husbands in every thing. Nevertheless let every one of you in particular so love his wife even as himself; and the wife see that she reverence her husband." Ephesians 5:24, 33.

"Likewise, ye wives, be in subjection to your own husbands; that, if any obey not the word, they also may without the word be won by the conversation of the wives." 1 Peter 3:1.

11. Should this be considered an inferior position?

A. No. For it is exactly the same as Christ takes to His Father.

"But I would have you know, that the head of every man is Christ; and the head of the woman is the man; and the head of Christ is God." 1 Corinthians 11:3.

12. Are not husband and wife equal?

A. Yes. They are one even as God and Christ are one.

"And they twain shall be one flesh: so then they are no more twain, but one flesh." Mark 10:8.

"I and my Father are one." John 10:30.

13. Wherein is this relation proper and perfect?

A. As the Father loves the Son and gives Him all that He has, so the man loves his wife and gives her all that he has. In both cases, love produces love and this results in unending peace and happiness.

VII. Duties to Children

1. What is the first duty of parents to their children?

A. The first duty of parents to their children is to bring them up in the nurture and admonition of the Lord.

"And, ye fathers, provoke not your children to wrath: but bring them up in the nurture and admonition of the Lord." Ephesians 6:4.

2. What does this involve?

A. This involves, first of all, faithfully teaching them the Word of God.

"And thou shalt teach them diligently unto thy children, and shalt talk of them when thou sittest in thine house, and when thou walkest by the way, and when thou liest down, and when thou risest up." Deuteronomy 6:7.

"Whom shall he teach knowledge? and whom shall he make to understand doctrine? them that are weaned from the milk, and drawn from the breasts. For precept must be upon precept, precept upon precept; line upon line, line upon line; here a little, and there a little." Isaiah 28:9-10.

3. What else is included in this command?

A. The training of the child in the way which he should go is also included in this command.

"Train up a child in the way he should go: and when he is old, he will not depart from it." Proverbs 22:6.

"He that spareth his rod hateth his son: but he that loveth him chasteneth him betimes." Proverbs 13:24.

4. Cite an excellent practice for the spiritual culture of children.

A. The family altar.

"And thou shalt teach them diligently unto thy children, and shalt talk of them when thou sittest in thine house, and when thou walkest by the way, and when thou liest down, and when thou risest up." Deuteronomy 6:7.

5. What is meant by the family altar?

A. It is the practice of parents' calling their family together daily (preferably twice daily, morning and night) for Scripture reading and prayer. The father (or the mother, if the father cannot function) will read a portion of the Bible (not too short or too long) and will lead in prayer. All members of the family could take turns reading one or two verses each and then take turns in prayer. This holy practice puts God at the beginning and end of each day and sows the seed of the Word in children's hearts. It is a blessed and effective means of bringing children up in the nurture and admonition of the Lord.

VIII. Duties to the Government

1. What is the relation of a Christian to the country in which he lives?

A. He is a citizen or a subject as his neighbors are.

"Let every soul be subject unto the higher powers. For there is no power but of God: the powers that be are ordained of God." Romans 13:1.

2. Does he belong to another country as well?

A. Yes. He belongs to a heavenly country. His citizenship is in heaven.

"For our conversation is in heaven: from whence

also we look for the Saviour, the Lord Jesus Christ."
Philippians 3:20.

3. How does this affect his earthly citizenship?

A. Only to subordinate it to the claims of his heavenly citizenship.

"Jesus said unto him, Thou shalt love the Lord thy God with all thy heart, and with all thy soul, and with all thy mind." Matthew 22:37.

4. What are his specific duties to the government under which he lives?

A. His duty first of all is to cause that prayers, supplications, intercessions and giving of thanks be made for kings and for all that are in authority.

"I exhort therefore, that, first of all, supplications, prayers, intercessions, and giving of thanks, be made for all men; for kings, and for all that are in authority; that we may lead a quiet and peaceable life in all godliness and honesty." 1 Timothy 2:1-2.

5. What else must he do?

A. He must honor the king, or the highest public office in the land. This would involve respect in measure, for all governmental officials.

"Honour all men. Love the brotherhood. Fear God. Honour the king." 1 Peter 2:17.

6. How is this respect to be shown?

A. This respect should be shown by being subject to higher powers and submitting himself to every ordinance of man for the Lord's sake; whether it be to the king as supreme; or unto governors, as unto them that are sent by him for the punishment of evildoers.

"Let every soul be subject unto the higher powers. For there is no power but of God: the powers that be are ordained of God." Romans 13:1.

"Submit yourselves to every ordinance of man for the

Lord's sake: whether it be to the king, as supreme;
or unto governors, as unto them that are sent by him
for the punishment of evildoers, and for the praise
of them that do well." 1 Peter 2:13-14.

7. Does this mean obedience to all laws, such as speed laws, and the payment of all taxes?

A. Yes, for the payment of tribute is specially mentioned.

"And when they were come to Capernaum, they that
received tribute money came to Peter, and said, Doth
not your master pay tribute? He saith, Yes. And when
he was come into the house, Jesus prevented him, saying, What thinkest thou, Simon? of whom do the kings
of the earth take custom or tribute? of their own
children, or of strangers? Peter saith unto him, Of
strangers. Jesus saith unto him, Then are the children
free. Notwithstanding, lest we should offend them
go thou to the sea, and cast an hook, and take up
the fish that first cometh up; and when thou hast
opened his mouth, thou shalt find a piece of money:
that take, and give unto them for me and thee."
Matthew 17:24-27.

"Render therefore to all their dues: tribute to whom
tribute is due; custom to whom custom; fear to whom
fear; honour to whom honour." Romans 13:7.

8. Is capital punishment right?

A. Yes, for it is scriptural. In both the Old and
the New Testament it is commanded or approved.

"Whoso sheddeth man's blood, by man shall his blood
be shed: for in the image of God made he man."
Genesis 9:6.

"For he is the minister of God to thee for good.
But if thou do that which is evil, be afraid; for he
beareth not the sword in vain: for he is the minister
of God, a revenger to execute wrath upon him that
doeth evil." Romans 13:4.

**9. Is taking life as an agent of the government then ac-
counted as murder in God's sight?**

A. No, for it is in obedience to the powers that be
and as their agent, rather than as an individual out of revenge or anger.

IX. Duties of Employers and Employees

**1. Does God approve of the employer-employee relation-
ship?**

A. Yes, for He nowhere condemns it, and gives
it tacit approval by giving instructions gov-
erning it.

"Servants, be obedient to them that are your masters
according to the flesh, with fear and trembling, in
singleness of your heart, as unto Christ." Ephesians 6:5.

**2. What is the right attitude of a Christian employer to
his employees?**

A. He will remember that he also has an Employer in heaven who will deal with him as
he deals with them; that he is himself a
servant of Christ.

"And, ye masters, do the same things unto them,
forbearing threatening: knowing that your Master
also is in heaven; neither is there respect of persons
with him." Ephesians 6:9.

3. What is the duty of the employer to the employee?

A. He should not threaten or be overbearing
toward them but should rather be just and
impartial and show good will in his relation
to them.

"Masters, give unto your servants that which is just
and equal; knowing that ye also have a Master in
heaven." Colossians 4:1.

**4. What practice of some employers is cited as a sign
of the last days?**

A. Keeping back by fraud of the wages of those
who have worked for them is cited as a sign
of the last days in James 5:3-4.

"Your gold and silver is cankered; and the rust of them shall be a witness against you, and shall eat your flesh as it were fire. Ye have heaped treasure together for the last days. Behold, the hire of the labourers who have reaped down your fields, which is of you kept back by fraud, crieth: and the cries of them which have reaped are entered into the ears of the Lord of Sabaoth." James 5:3-4.

5. How should a Christian employee work for his employer?

A. He should work for his employer as if he were working for Christ himself. This is emphasized in Ephesians 6:5-8 and should be taken literally and seriously.

"Servants, be obedient to them that are your masters according to the flesh, with fear and trembling, in singleness of your heart, as unto Christ; Not with eyeservice, as menpleasers; but as the servants of Christ, doing the will of God from the heart; With good will doing service, as to the Lord, and not to men. Knowing that whatsoever good thing any man doeth, the same shall he receive of the Lord, whether he be bond or free." Ephesians 6:5-8.

6. Should advantage be taken of a Christian employer because he is a brother in the Lord?

A. No. This is specifically warned against in 1 Timothy 6:2.

"And they that have believing masters, let them not despise them, because they are brethren; but rather do them service, because they are faithful and beloved, partakers of the benefit. These things teach and exhort." 1 Timothy 6:2.

7. Should any distinction be made between good and bad employers?

A. No distinction should be made between good and bad employers.

"Servants, be subject to your masters with all fear; not only to the good and gentle, but also to the froward. For this is thankworthy, if a man for conscience toward God endure grief, suffering wrongfully. For what glory is it, if, when ye be buffeted for your faults, ye shall take it patiently? but if, when ye do well, and suffer for it, ye take it patiently, this is acceptable with God." 1 Peter 2:18-20.

X. Duty to Neighbors

1. What is the second greatest commandment?

A. "Thou shalt love thy neighbor as thyself." Matthew 22:39.

2. Wherein is this such an important commandment?

A. Because all detailed commandments such as "Thou shalt not steal, Thou shalt not kill, Thou shalt not bear false witness," etc., are briefly comprehended in the one commandment, "Thou shalt love thy neighbor as thyself." Romans 13:9.

"Love worketh no ill to his neighbor; therefore love is the fulfilling of the law." Romans 13:10.

3. What is the practical result of keeping this commandment?

A. It will result in a friendliness, a kindly helpfulness and a consideration of the interests of our neighbors.

4. To what extent should this consideration go?

A. We should do unto others as we want them to do to us.

"Therefore all things whatsoever ye would that men should do to you, do ye even so to them: for this is the law and the prophets." Matthew 7:12.

5. Is this natural neighborliness all that is included in the scope of this commandment?

A. No. As we are interested in the welfare of our own souls, we should also be interested in the spiritual welfare of our neighbors.

6. And who is our neighbor?

A. Jesus answered this question by giving the parable of the Good Samaritan. Anyone anywhere who is in need is our neighbor.

"But he, willing to justify himself, said unto Jesus, And who is my neighbour? And Jesus answering said, A certain man went down from Jerusalem to Jericho, and fell among thieves, which stripped him of his raiment, and wounded him, and departed, leaving him half dead. And by chance there came down a certain priest that way: and when he saw him, he passed by on the other side. And likewise a Levite, when he was at the place, came and looked on him, and passed by on the other side. But a certain Samaritan, as he journeyed, came where he was: and when he saw him, he had compassion on him, and went to him, and bound up his wounds, pouring in oil and wine, and set him on his own beast, and brought him to an inn, and took care of him. And on the morrow when he departed, he took out two pence, and gave them to the host, and said unto him, Take care of him; and whatsoever thou spendest more, when I come again, I will repay thee. Which now of these three, thinkest thou, was neighbour unto him that fell among the thieves? And he said, He that shewed mercy on him. Then said Jesus unto him, Go, and do thou likewise." Luke 10:29-37.

XI. Duties to the World

1. What is meant by "the world"?

A. The word "world" in the Bible refers to the world system which is an enemy to God. It also means "all the earth" or, all people.

"Love not the world, neither the things that are in the world. If any man love the world, the love of the Father is not in him." 1 John 2:15.

"And he said unto them, Go ye into all the world, and preach the gospel to every creature." Mark 16:15.

2. What should the Christian's attitude be toward the world system?

A. He should separate himself in spirit from everything worldly.

"Ye adulterers and adulteresses, know ye not that the friendship of the world is enmity with God? whosoever therefore will be a friend of the world is the enemy of God." James 4:4.

"Love not the world, neither the things that are in the world. If any man love the world, the love of the Father is not in him. For all that is in the world, the lust of the flesh, and the lust of the eyes, and the pride of life, is not of the Father, but is of the world. And the world passeth away, and the lust thereof: but he that doeth the will of God abideth forever." 1 John 2:15-17.

3. What should the Christian's attitude be toward all people of the world?

A. Christians should love the world as their heavenly Father does.

"For God so loved the world, that he gave his only begotten Son, that whosoever believeth in him should not perish, but have everlasting life." John 3:16.

They are also commanded to go into all the world and preach the gospel to every creature.

"And he said unto them, Go ye into all the world, and preach the gospel to every creature." Mark 16:15.

4. How does this affect individual Christians?

A. Each Christian must find out from the Lord what part of the "world" he must go into with the gospel. He may go across the street or into the highways and hedges of his own city. But all Christians must go somewhere with the gospel.

"For the Son of man is as a man taking a far journey, who left his house, and gave authority to his servants, and to every man his work, and commanded the porter to watch." Mark 13:34.

5. What did Jesus declare in the Sermon on the Mount was the Christian's relation to the world?

A. He said, "Ye are the salt of the earth" and "Ye are the light of the world."

> "Ye are the salt of the earth: but if the salt have lost his savour, wherewith shall it be salted? it is henceforth good for nothing, but to be cast out, and to be trodden under foot of men. Ye are the light of the world. A city that is set on an hill cannot be hid." Matthew 5:13-14.

6. What did He say was the Christian's duty toward the world?

A. He said, "Let your light so shine before men, that they may see your good works, and glorify your Father which is in heaven." Matthew 5:16.

XII. Duties to Oneself

1. What is the first law of nature?

A. Self-preservation is the first law of nature.

2. Is this a law of the kingdom of God?

A. No. The opposite is true in the kingdom of God. Self-denial and humbling oneself are the prerequisite and essence of spiritual life.

> "And he said to them all, If any man will come after me, let him deny himself, and take up his cross daily, and follow me." Luke 9:23.
> "And whosoever shall exalt himself shall be abased; and he that shall humble himself shall be exalted." Matthew 23:12.

3. What is the corresponding law of the kingdom of God?

A. "He that loveth his life shall lose it; and he that hateth his life in this world shall keep it unto life eternal." John 12:25.

4. What is the first duty of a Christian to himself?

A. To present his body a living sacrifice to God and to yield his members as instruments of righteousness unto God.

"I beseech you therefore, brethren, by the mercies of God, that ye present your bodies a living sacrifice, holy, acceptable unto God, which is your reasonable service." Romans 12:1.

"Neither yield ye your members as instruments of unrighteousness unto sin: but yield yourselves unto God, as those that are alive from the dead, and your members as instruments of righteousness unto God." Romans 6:13.

5. What is the supreme objective of a Christian's life?

A. To be accepted of Christ.

"Wherefore we labour, that, whether present or absent, we may be accepted of him." 2 Corinthians 5:9.

"His lord said unto him, Well done, thou good and faithful servant: thou hast been faithful over a few things, I will make thee ruler over many things: enter thou into the joy of thy lord." Matthew 25:21.

B. BOOK STUDIES

I. Pauline Epistles
ROMANS

1. What is the theme of the book of Romans?

A. The gift of righteousness is the theme of the book of Romans. Paul says in Romans 1:16 and 17 that he is not ashamed of the gospel of Christ, . . . "for therein is the righteousness of God revealed."

2. What is the need for this gift of righteousness to the human race?

A. The gift of righteousness is needed because all have sinned, both Jews and Gentiles, and have come short of the glory of God.

"For all have sinned, and come short of the glory of God." Romans 3:23.

3. How was it possible for a just God to impute righteousness to sinful people?

A. He made propitiation for their sins through the substitutionary death of His Son, and then by grace freely justifies them who believe in Jesus Christ.

"Being justified freely by his grace through the redemption that is in Christ Jesus: Whom God hath set forth to be a propitiation through faith in his blood, to declare his righteousness for the remission of sins that are past, through the forbearance of God; To declare, I say, at this time his righteousness: that he might be just, and the justifier of him which believeth in Jesus." Romans 3:24-26.

4. What is God's plan for imparting righteousness to believers?

A. Christ took man's sinful nature ("the old man") to the cross with Him, and believers are invited to accept this deliverance. They must reckon themselves dead unto sin and refuse to yield their members as instruments of unrighteousness unto sin. Instead they must reckon themselves alive unto God and yield their members as instruments of righteousness unto God. Thus God's righteousness is actually imparted to believers and is manifested in mortal flesh.

"Knowing this, that our old man is crucified with him, that the body of sin might be destroyed, that henceforth we should not serve sin. . . . Let not sin therefore reign in your mortal body, that ye should obey it in the lusts thereof. Neither yield ye your members as instruments of unrighteousness unto sin: but yield yourselves unto God, as those that are alive from the dead, and your members as instruments of righteousness unto God." Romans 6:6, 12, 13.

5. What is the secret of complete victory in Christian living?

A. The presence and power of the Holy Spirit in the Christian's life.

"There is therefore now no condemnation to them which are in Christ Jesus, who walk not after the flesh, but after the Spirit. For the law of the Spirit of life in Christ Jesus hath made me free from the law of sin and death . . . and if Christ be in you, the body is dead because of sin; but the Spirit is life because of righteousness." Romans 8:1, 2, 10.

6. What manifestation of God's righteousness is expected in a Christian's life?

A. In the operation of the gifts of the Spirit, in practical holiness, in loyalty to the government under which one lives, and in consideration and respect for fellow Christians. Romans 12 to 14.

7. What is the place of the Jews in God's plan of redemption?

A. They received God's oracles in the first place, and from the Jews came the prophets and Christ Himself. By their rejection of Christ blindness in part happened to them, but eventually they will be brought back into favor with God. Romans 9 to 11.

1 CORINTHIANS

1. What does the Epistle of 1 Corinthians teach about the wisdom of man?

A. 1 Corinthians teaches that man's wisdom is insufficient and comes to naught, but that Christ is made unto us the wisdom of God and by God's redemption we have the mind of Christ.

"But of him are ye in Christ Jesus, who of God is made unto us wisdom, and righteousness, and sanctification, and redemption." 1 Corinthians 1:30.

2. What is the law of Christian marriage and divorce as set forth in this epistle?

A. Christians should marry only Christians, and divorced Christians should remain unmarried as long as their companions live.

"The wife is bound by the law as long as her husband liveth; but if her husband be dead, she is at liberty to be married to whom she will; only in the Lord." 1 Corinthians 7:39.

3. What are some facts about the gifts of the Spirit which Paul presents in chapters 12 to 14?

A. (1) They are distributed by the *Holy Ghost* to each person according to His own will.

"But all these worketh that one and the selfsame Spirit, dividing to every man severally as he will." 1 Corinthians 12:11.

(2) A person should not minimize his gift. Cf. 1 Corinthians 12:18-26.

(3) A person should not over-value his gift.

"But covet earnestly the best gifts: and yet shew I unto you a more excellent way." 1 Corinthians 12:31.

(4) There is a graded rank of position and ministries in the Body of Christ.

"For as the body is one, and hath many members, and all the members of that one body, being many, are one body: so also is Christ. . . . And God hath set some in the church, first apostles, secondarily prophets, thirdly teachers, after that miracles, then gifts of healings, helps, governments, diversities of tongues." 1 Corinthians 12:12, 28.

by love.
(5) Gifts are of no value if not controlled

"Though I speak with the tongues of men and of angels, and have not charity, I am become as sounding brass, or a tinkling cymbal. Though I have the gift of prophecy, and understand all mysteries, and all knowledge; and though I have all faith, so that I could remove mountains, and have not charity, I am nothing. And though I bestow all my goods to feed the poor, and though I give my body to be burned, and have not charity, it profiteth me nothing." 1 Corinthians 13:1-3.

(6) Prophecy is the most desirable gift.

"Follow after charity, and desire spiritual gifts, but rather that ye may prophesy. For he that speaketh in an unknown tongue speaketh not unto men, but unto God: for no man understandeth him; howbeit in the spirit he speaketh mysteries. But he that prophesieth speaketh unto men to edification, and exhortation, and comfort. He that speaketh in an unknown tongue edifieth himself; but he that prophesieth edifieth the church. I would that ye all spake with tongues, but rather that ye prophesied, for greater is he that prophesieth than he that speaketh with tongues. except he interpret, that the church may receive edifying. Wherefore, brethren covet to prophesy, and forbid not to speak with tongues." 1 Corinthians 14:1-5, 39.

(7) Tongues spoken in a church service
should always be interpreted.

"If there be no interpreter, let him keep silence in the
church: and let him speak to himself, and to God."
1 Corinthians 14:28.

(8) Messages in prophecy or in tongues
should not exceed three in one service.

"If any man speak in an unknown tongue, let it be
by two, or at the most by three, and that by course;
and let one interpret. . . . Let the prophets speak
two or three, and let the other judge." 1 Corinthians
14:27, 29.

(9) Manifestation of the gifts should not be
forbidden, but rather encouraged.

"But the manifestation of the Spirit is given to every
man to profit withal." 1 Corinthians 12:7.
"Even so ye, forasmuch as ye are zealous of spiritual
gifts, seek that ye may excel to the edifying of the
church." 1 Corinthians 14:12. Cf. 1 Corinthians
14:39; 1 Thessalonians 5:19.

(10) The operation of all the gifts should
serve to edify the church. Cf. 1 Corinthians 12:7; 14:1-5, 12.

**4. What is the nature and importance of love as set
forth in 1 Corinthians 13?**

A. Love is self-effacing and others-exalting. It
is the very life-stream of the effective operation of the gifts of the Spirit and of all worth-
while sacrifice and philanthropy. It will out-
last all gifts and virtues and is greater even
than hope and faith.

**5. Why does 1 Corinthians 15 present the resurrection
of Christ as the greatest Christian doctrine?**

A. If Christ be not risen we would still be in
our sins, for God showed His acceptance of

Christ's sacrifice for our sins by raising Him from the dead.

"And if Christ be not raised, your faith is vain; ye are yet in your sins." 1 Corinthians 15:17.

6. What does this chapter teach is the nature of the resurrection of Christians?

A. There are two phases to the resurrection:

(1) As a grain of corn planted in the ground decays before coming up in the spring, so a deceased Christian's body decomposes; but at the resurrection, God will bring forth a new glorified body similar in physical likeness to the old. The resurrected body is raised incorruptible.

(2) At the time of the resurrection there will be those who are alive on the earth. These "mortals" will be changed. They will "put on" immortality, while the dead will be raised incorruptible.

"Behold, I shew you a mystery; We shall not all sleep, but we shall all be changed, In a moment, in the twinkling of an eye, at the last trump; for the trumpet shall sound, and the dead shall be raised incorruptible, and we shall be changed. For this corruptible must put on incorruption, and this mortal must put on immortality. So when this corruptible shall have put on incorruption, and this mortal shall have put on immortality, then shall be brought to pass the saying that is written, Death is swallowed up in victory." 1 Corinthians 15:51-54. Cf. 1 Corinthians 15:35-38.

2 CORINTHIANS—GALATIANS

1. What is the over-all theme of 2 Corinthians?

A. Paul explains and defends his apostleship.

2. What are some other important teachings of this book?

A. The Judgment seat of Christ (5:10) and Christian giving. Chapters 8 and 9.

3. What is the theme of the book of Galatians?

A. Justification by faith apart from law or works of any kind.

"... No man is justified by the law in the sight of God, it is evident: for, The just shall live by faith." Galatians 3:11.

4. How does Paul present and prove justification by faith?

A. He proves it by citing:

(1) The fact that the Galatians themselves had received the Spirit by faith and not by the works of the law:

(2) That Abraham received his righteousness by believing God (3:6);

(3) That Christ had borne the curse of the law for us and by accepting Him we inherit the blessing of Abraham through Christ who is Abraham's seed.

5. What practical life-results will follow if we stand fast in the liberty of the gospel of faith and walk in the Spirit?

A. The fruits of the Spirit will appear in our lives; such as love, joy, peace, longsuffering, gentleness, goodness, faith, meekness, and temperance.

"But the fruit of the Spirit is love, joy, peace, longsuffering, gentleness, goodness, faith, meekness, temperance: against such there is no law." Galatians 5: 22, 23.

EPHESIANS—PHILIPPIANS

1. What is the theme of Ephesians?

A. The theme of this book is the position and walk of the Church.

2. What is here taught about the position of the Church?

A. Chosen in Him before the foundation of the world, the Church has been potentially resurrected with Christ and is now set down with Him in heavenly places, far above principalities and powers.

3. What does this epistle teach concerning the walk of the Church?

A. Putting off the old man, the Church should walk in love and righteousness in the new man, being filled with the Spirit and praying in the Spirit.

4. What is the keynote and theme of Philippians?

A. The keynote is rejoice, and the theme is Christian experience and fellowship. 3:1.

5. In what varying Christian experiences does Paul rejoice and call upon the Philippians to rejoice?

A. In the gospel's being preached, in suffering for His sake, in sacrifice and service, and in the Lord alway.

6. What four examples of beautiful Christian living are set forth in this epistle?

A. Of Christ, of Timothy, of Epaphroditus, and of Paul himself.

COLOSSIANS

1. Compare the epistle of Colossians with Ephesians.

A. Both record apostolic prayers, both exalt Christ as the head of the Church, both declare the believer's identification with Christ, both speak of the old man and the new man, and both exhort husbands and wives, parents and children, masters, and servants.

2. What material is found in Colossians exclusively?

A. The warnings against philosophy, legalism, mysticism and asceticism.

"Beware lest any many spoil you through philosophy and vain deceit, after the tradition of men, after the rudiments of the world, and not after Christ. . . . Blotting out the handwriting of ordinances that was against us, which was contrary to us, and took it out of the way, nailing it to his cross. . . . Let no man beguile you of your reward in a voluntary humility and worshipping of angels, intruding into those things which he hath not seen, vainly puffed up by his fleshly mind. . . . Which things have indeed a shew of wisdom in will worship, and humility, and neglecting of the body; not in any honour to the satisfying of the flesh." Colossians 2:8, 14, 18, 23.

3. How were these errors answered?

A. Christ is the absolute and ultimate in truth; the ordinances were nailed with Him on the cross; and death and resurrection with Christ remove us from the need of vague speculation and bodily penance.

"If ye then be risen with Christ, seek those things which are above, where Christ sitteth on the right hand of God. Set your affection on things above, not on things on the earth. For ye are dead, and your life is hid with Christ in God." Colossians 3:1-3.

1 AND 2 THESSALONIANS

1. What is the dominant theme of 1 and 2 Thessalonians?

A. The second coming of Christ.

2. What division of this theme do these epistles make?

A. 1 Thessalonians describes the rapture of the

saints as taking place before "the day of the Lord" (the tribulation and the revelation of Christ); and 2 Thessalonians describes the career of the Antichrist who will be revealed after the church is taken out of the way.

1 AND 2 TIMOTHY AND TITUS

1. Why are these three epistles called the Pastoral Epistles?

A. Because they consist chiefly of instructions given to pastors.

2. What were some of these instructions?

A. The standard qualifications for the ministry and for the diaconate are here given in detail. Public prayer for government officials is enjoined. Advice is also given concerning the importance of Bible study, and of purity and vigilance in personal matters.

3. What indication appears that these were among the last epistles which Paul wrote?

A. They contain many warnings concerning conditions which would exist in the last days. Paul wrote that many would depart from the faith and teach fables, being satisfied with a mere form of godliness. They would even give heed to seducing spirits and doctrines of devils (demons).

PHILEMON

What is the special characteristic of the book of Philemon?

A. It not only reveals the high ethics and gracious manner of Paul the aged, but it provides a beautiful illustration of how Christ, who loves us undeserving sinners, has declared, "Put his sins on my account, I will repay."

II. General Epistles
1. Why is this first general epistle called "Hebrews"?

A. Because it was doubtless written to the Jewish people and because its message is an argument concerning the superiority of Christianity to Judaism.

2. What are the main points of this argument?

A. That Christ, the Founder of Christianity, is superior to the prophets, who proclaimed Judaism; superior to the angels, who ministered to Israel; superior to Moses, who was the great teacher and founder of Judaism; and superior to Aaron, the first High Priest of Israel; and that the new covenant is better than the Mosaic covenant.

3. What is the outstanding chapter of the book of Hebrews?

A. The eleventh, because it gives the list of the Old Testament worthies who attained their high place with God by *faith*.

4. For what is the book of James remarkable?

A. For its emphasis on works as necessary to manifest and prove the reality of faith.

5. What is the key word of 1 Peter?

A. The key word of 1 Peter is "suffering," for throughout the epistle the sufferings of Christ are cited as an example to Christians, that we "should follow his steps."

6. What is the particular message of 2 Peter?

A. The message of 2 Peter is warning concerning the false teachers who will bring in damnable heresies in the last days. A description of the Day of the Lord is also given in chapter 3.

7. What does John give as the purpose of his first epistle?

A. The purpose of 1 John is to promote fellowship with God. Cf. 1 John 1:3-7.

8. What characteristics of God are cited to which we must conform in order to have fellowship with Him?

A. These characteristics are: light (1 John 1:5), righteousness (2:29), and love (4:7, 8).

9. Why did Jude consider it necessary to "contend earnestly for the faith"?

A. He contended for the faith in order to resist the attack and the undermining tactics of certain men who "turn the grace of God into lasciviousness," who "run greedily after reward" and who "despise dominion and speak evil of dignities." vv. 4, 8, 11.

III. Poetical Books

1. Which books of the Bible are called the Poetical Books?

A. Job, Psalms, Proverbs, Ecclesiastes and the Song of Solomon are called the Poetical books, for they are a collection of Hebrew poems.

2. What are the general contents and the purpose of the book of Job?

A. The book of Job is the story of a man of God who suffered the loss of all material wealth, and family, and also suffered great physical pain. The purpose is to provide an answer to the eternal question as to why the Lord allows loss and suffering to come to His own righteous children.

3. What is the answer to this question provided by the book of Job?

A. The answer is threefold:

  (1) To purify Christian hearts from the dross of self-righteousness;

  (2) To demonstrate God's sovereignty and right to act in ways beyond the power of man to comprehend;

  (3) To display to principalities and powers the wonders of His grace sufficient to enable a man to love and trust God for God's own sake and without evident compensation for doing so.

PSALMS

1. Who wrote the Psalms?

A. David wrote about half of them and others are ascribed to Asaph, Korah, Moses and Solomon; and many are anonymous.

2. What is the general character of the Psalms?

A. They express the emotions and true heart feelings of their authors.   They were the hymns of Jewish worship.

3. Is there prophetic significance in any of the Psalms?

A. Yes. Certain Psalms are Messianic.   They refer to the coming Messiah, and are actually the secret prayers and heart reaction of the Messiah revealed a thousand years in advance. Among these, Psalm 22 concerning the crucifixion, and Psalm 16 concerning the resur‑ rection are outstanding.

4. What other future events are predicted in the Psalms?

A. The part which Judas played in Jesus' life is shown in Psalm 41:9; 55:12-13; 69:25 and

109:1-20. Knowledge of these scriptures doubtless led and strengthened Jesus in His choice of Judas and in His enduring His betrayal by him. John 6:64; Matthew 26:47-50. There are also Psalms which describe Armageddon and the Millennium; e. g., Psalms 2 and 72.

5. What is unique about the 119th Psalm?

A. It is an acrostic, each section beginning with a successive letter of the Hebrew alphabet. Also it is the longest chapter in the Bible, and every one of its 176 verses contains some reference to the Word of God.

PROVERBS

1. Who is the author, and what is the nature of the book of Proverbs?

A. Solomon, the son of David, is the author of this book which is a collection of terse sentences containing concentrated moral truth. These proverbs usually state contrasts of truth, giving the good and bad aspects.

2. Is it natural or spiritual truth which is presented in the book of Proverbs?

A. Both are presented. Outstanding examples of spiritual truth are found in 1:7; 3:5-6; 4:18, 23; 11:24; 14:12, 14 and 18:10.

ECCLESIASTES

What are the key phrases of the book of Ecclesiastes?

A. "Under the sun" and "vanity of vanities." This book is therefore a treatise concerning earthly, or natural, life (under the sun) and the teaching is that all "under the sun" is "vanity of vanities."

THE SONG OF SOLOMON

What is the nature of The Song of Solomon? Does it have a spiritual significance?

A. It is the love story of an oriental king, and it typifies the love of Christ and His church.

IV. The Major Prophets

ISAIAH

1. When did Isaiah live and of whom did he prophesy?

A. Isaiah lived during the reigns of Uzziah (10th from Solomon), Ahaz, Jotham and Hezekiah, kings of Judah. He prophesied from about 760 to 700 B.C. primarily to the Jews who lived in the southern kingdom at that time.

2. What is unusual about the chapter divisions of his books?

A. The prophecy of Isaiah, like the Bible itself, has 66 chapters (or books) and there is a distinct break after the first 39 chapters. This corresponds with the 39 books of the Old Testament and the 27 of the New Testament.

3. What is distinctive about Isaiah's prophecy?

A. He is called the evangelist of the Old Testament because his description of Calvary in the fifty-third chapter is the most vivid of all Old Testament prophecies of the suffering Messiah and His redemptive work. This is especially significant since the contents of Isaiah, chapters 40-66, predict Israel's restoration from Babylon, and her still future final restoration, because of the atoning death and later exaltation of her Messiah, our Lord Jesus Christ.

JEREMIAH

1. When did Jeremiah live and what were the conditions under which he prophesied?

A. Jeremiah lived about 100 years after Isaiah and prophesied at the time when Judah was being taken captive. Some of his later prophecies were made in the land of Egypt where he had accompanied the Jewish remnant who had fled from the king of Babylon.

2. Why is Jeremiah called the "Weeping Prophet"?

A. Because of his expressed great sorrow for the willful, doomed Jewish nation. The book of Lamentations contains some of the sorrowful utterances of Jeremiah for his people.

3. Was Jeremiah popular and were his warnings and prophecies obeyed by the people?

A. No. Kings, nobles, priests and people angrily rejected his counsel and threw him into prison, once into a dungeon.

4. But did his prophecies come true?

A. Yes. The city of Jerusalem fell to the Babylonians as Jeremiah said it would. His prophecies concerning the future "time of Jacob's trouble" and their final blessing in the land of Palestine will also come true.

EZEKIEL

1. When did Ezekiel prophesy?

A. Ezekiel was carried away captive from Jerusalem into Babylon in 598 B.C. and wrote his prophecies there. The prophecies of the first twenty-four chapters were delivered during the reign of Jehoiachin before the destruction of Jerusalem.

2. What is the meaning of Ezekiel's vision of the valley of dry bones?

A. This vision is a graphic revelation of the national resurrection and restoration to Palestine of the Jewish nation in the last days.

3. What prophecy of Ezekiel's concerns a leading nation of the world at this time?

A. The prophecy of chapters 38 and 39 tells of Russia's invasion of Palestine in the latter days and of her destruction there.

DANIEL

1. What is contained in the book of Daniel?

A. It is a record of certain revelations of future events which God gave to him while he served in the court of Babylonian and Persian kings. Its scope is "the times of the Gentiles."

2. Do any of these revelations affect us today?

A. Yes. Daniel saw and described the successive world empires, including the anti-Christian one soon to be formed and the Millennial empire of Christ which is not far away,

3. What did Daniel prophesy concerning the Jews?

A. He said that they would be terribly persecuted in "the time of the end" by the Antichrist for three and one-half years, but that Michael the archangel would come to their defense and Christ Himself would destroy their persecutor and set up His own kingdom in the earth.

V. The Minor Prophets

1. What is peculiar about the book of Hosea?

A. Hosea is peculiar in that it tells of God's commanding His prophet to marry an unchaste woman, to have children by her to whom were given names with meaning for Israel; and then to be true to her when she deserted him for a life of shame. This was all an object lesson to show God's love for undeserving Israel even after she had deserted Him.

2. What is the theme of the book of Joel?

A. Joel speaks of the Day of the Lord as a time of the outpouring of the Spirit, a time when there will be great phenomena in nature and a time when the Lord will smite all nations who have persecuted His people Israel.

3 Who was Amos and how did he prophesy?

A. Amos was a herdsman and a gatherer of sycamore fruit, but God sent him to prophesy to Israel stern words of warning and judgment. These words were followed by a short but beautiful description of the fruitfulness of the Jewish people in the millennium. Amos 9:11-15.

4. Which is the shortest book in the Old Testament?

A. Obadiah uses but 23 verses to describe the sin of the nation of Edom (Esau's descendants) and to predict God's punishment of them in the day of the Lord.

5. What lessons are taught in the book of Jonah?

A. (1) That it doesn't pay to run away from God;

(2) That God controls the elements to perform His will; and

(3) That God will forgive even the vilest sinners if they only repent.

6. For what prophecy concerning the birth of Christ is the book of Micah famous?

A. "But thou, Bethlehem Ephratah, though thou be little among the thousands of Judah, yet out of thee shall he come forth unto me that is to be ruler in Israel; whose goings forth have been from of old, from everlasting." Micah 5:2.

7. What is the relation of the books of Nahum and Jonah?

A. They are both prophecies concerning Nineveh. Nahum's pronouncement (100 years later than Jonah's) was final, for Nineveh did not repent at his preaching.

8. What Gospel truth proclaimed by Habakkuk was quoted three times in the New Testament?

A. "The just shall live by his faith." Habakkuk 2:4; Romans 1:17; Galatians 3:11; Hebrews 10:38.

9. What was the burden of Zephaniah's message?

A. Zephaniah's message concerning the Day of the Lord called upon Israel to return to Palestine before that day came. Zephaniah 2:1.

10. When did Haggai prophesy?

A. Haggai was the first of the prophets who appeared after the return of the Jews from exile in Babylon. He encouraged the Jews to proceed at once with the rebuilding of the temple.

11. Who was Haggai's partner in prophesying?

A. Zechariah supported Haggai in his encouragement of Zerubbabel to depend upon God's

Spirit rather than upon human might or power.

"Then he answered and spake unto me, saying, This is the word of the Lord unto Zerubbabel, saying, Not by might, nor by power, but by my spirit, saith the Lord of hosts." Zechariah 4:6.

12. Who was the last of the Old Testament prophets?

A. Malachi prophesied about 400 years before Christ. He rebuked the priests of Israel for profanation of the sacrificial order and exhorted the Jews among other things to bring all their tithes into the storehouse and thus to prove their God.

"Bring ye all the tithes into the store house, that there may be meat in mine house, and prove me now herewith, saith the Lord of hosts, if I will not open you the windows of heaven, and pour you out a blessing, that there shall not be room enough to receive it." Malachi 3:10.